OFFICIAL

RIVEN™

THE SEQUEL TO MYST®

PLAYER'S GUIDE

by William H. Keith, Jr. and Nina Barton

BRADY STAFF

Publisher
Lynn Zingraf

Editor-In-Chief
H. Leigh Davis

Title/Licensing Manager
David Waybright

Marketing Manager
Janet Cadoff

Acquisitions Editor
Debra McBride

CREDITS

Development Editor
David Cassady

Project Editor
Tim Cox

Screenshot Editor
Michael Owen

Book & Cover Designer
Carol Ann Stamile

Production Designer
Tina Trettin

LEGAL STUFF

Brady Publishing

An Imprint of Macmillan Digital Publishing USA

450 East 96th St., Suite 400

Indianapolis, Indiana 46240

ISBN: 1-56686-762-2

Library of Congress Catalog #: 97-070249

Printing Code: The rightmost double-digit number is the year of the book's printing; the right-most single-digit number is the number of the book's printing. For example, 97-1 shows that the first printing of the book occurred in 1997.

00 99 98 97   4 3 2 1

Manufactured in the United States of America.

TABLE OF CONTENTS

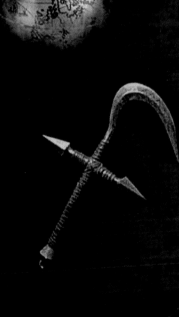

AUTHOR BIOS

William H. Keith, Jr.

As of this writing, Bill has written over 50 books and has several more in the pipeline, novels ranging from military technothrillers to military science fiction to science fiction comedy. Current series include Warstrider, an SF series under his own name, and SEALs: The Warrior Breed, a military historical-fiction series under the pseudonym H. Jay Riker. Before he started writing for a living, he was a professional SF illustrator and still occasionally exhibits his work at various cons and on the World Wide Web.

When he's not writing—is there such a time?—he can be found hiking, blowing holes in paper targets with firearms of various calibers, participating in Western Pennsylvania Mensa events, and hanging out with some very strange people. He lives in the mountains of western Pennsylvania with his wife, Nina.

Nina Barton

After years of editing Bill's prolific output, Nina Barton—alias Nina Keith—has begun writing on her own, probably out of sheer self defense. Unlike Bill, she understands both computers and computer people, a highly desirable talent when working on a game guide for BradyGAMES.

She is currently co-writing several novels with Bill. When she's able to pry herself away from the computer, she likes to hike, go to concerts, teach piano, shoot things, go to Mensa conventions, and hang around in bookstores. She lives with Bill in western Pennsylvania.

This is Bill and Nina's sixth book for BradyGAMES.

AUTHOR ACKNOWLEDGEMENTS

Any game guide like this one is of necessity a collaborative effort by many people. We would like to extend our special thanks, however, to Tim Cox, our editor at BradyGAMES, and to Brady's Acquisitions Editor Debra McBride, who made it all both possible and worthwhile.

And finally, our very special and sincere thanks to Cyan's Chris Brandkamp, who opened to us the mystical and wonderful universe that is Riven.

Chapter One

INTRODUCTION

Sunlight dances off an azure sea. You hear the cry of wheeling gulls overhead, the buzz and click of insects in the forest growth. You stand alone on the rocky shore of an island where, in the distance, you see strange and wonderful devices luring you forward with the promise of mystery and wonder. It has been long since you unlocked the puzzles of Myst Island and freed Atrus from the prison of D'ni. A new test, new challenges, face you now.

Welcome to the Fifth Age, and the mysterious world of Riven.

Riven is a complex and challenging game. Riven The Sequel to Myst Official Player's Guide is designed to allow you to work your way through each location within the Fifth Age...and make decisions for yourself. Do you want a word or two to push you in the right direction? Or do you want a step-by-step listing of the places you must go and the things you must do to crack each puzzle in turn.

VAGUE TO SPECIFIC: HOW MUCH DO YOU WANT TO KNOW?

Each chapter of this book is rated according to how little or how much it actually gives away. To understand the graphic symbols that warn of spoilers to the game, however, you need to take a quick look at a few of the creatures inhabiting the islands of Riven.

THE BEETLE

This is a small and harmless creature you may see flying about in the jungle or crawling on a log.

A picture of a Beetle appearing on the running headers of a chapter means that very little is given away in that section. There are no hints or solutions of any kind, although some of the background information may be generally useful in your quest.

THE FROG

You may or may not see a Frog in your wanderings. Frogs are harmless, but they're a step up on the food chain from Beetles.

A picture of a Frog appearing on the running headers of a chapter means that the section in question does contain hints, although no solutions are given away outright. Look in these chapters for subtle clues or a gentle nudge in the right direction.

THE SUNNER

You may, if you're lucky, encounter Sunners in Riven, bizarre, otherworldly creatures like improbable hybrids of penguins, baleen whales, and plesiosaurs. Sunners are decidedly larger than Frogs and much more mysterious.

A picture of a Sunner appearing on the running headers of a chapter means that this chapter gives away quite a bit. It stops short of telling you the solutions to the puzzles outright, but it will take you to the very brink of revelation. Don't look here if you'd rather figure out the puzzles for yourself!

THE WAHRK

You may never encounter one in your travels, but signs of the Wahrk's existence—and its importance to the world-islands of Riven—can be found everywhere. It is an aquatic beast, a melding of whale and shark, and it is undeniably dangerous.

A picture of a Wahrk in the running headers is a reminder that these chapters in the book give away everything. If you want to preserve any of the mystery and brain-teasing wonder of Riven and you come to this symbol, do not read any further!

CHAPTER BY CHAPTER:

RIVEN PLAYER'S GUIDE

Now that you've completed your lesson in Riven zoology, let's see how the chapters of this book are laid out.

CHAPTER 1: INTRODUCTION

This introduction to the game and the book gives away nothing of substance. It includes this description of the book's chapters and a section on how to use this book.

CHAPTER 2: ROAMING THROUGH RIVEN

This is a brief chapter that, again, gives away very little. It provides a quick look at the game controls and cursor types, and a brief overview of how to maneuver through the worlds of Riven.

CHAPTER 3: THE ISLANDS OF RIVEN: HINTS AND MUSINGS

This chapter is divided into seven sections, one for each of seven places you may visit in the course of your travels. Each section begins with a brief description of the place, followed by lists of hints and tips arranged top to bottom, from vague to more specific. The solutions to puzzles and problems are not given away outright, however. There are some things you still must work for!

CHAPTER 4: THE ISLANDS OF RIVEN: MAPS AND SPECIFICS

As in Chapter 3, this chapter is divided into sections describing each area within Riven. This time, however, each area is mapped out in detail; looking at a map of, say, Jungle Island will definitely give away some of the surprises, if only because you will know what's on the other side of that tunnel...or which direction on a forking path to choose in order to reach a particular control. Also included are lists of the puzzles and problems that must be solved for you to proceed through the game, along with some specific hints and tips for solving them.

Use this chapter carefully if you want to preserve the mystery and suspense of the rest of the game!

CHAPTER 5: PUZZLES AND PROBLEMS: THE SOLUTIONS

The Gate Room. The Gallows. The Star Fissure Window. This chapter lists each of the major puzzles and problems in the game and tells you how to solve them. Remember, though, that much of the joy of playing Riven comes from piecing together the subtle and widely scattered clues that enable you to reason out the answers for yourself. Please don't look in this chapter unless you're totally baffled and cannot solve the problem in any other way!

CHAPTER 6: WALKTHROUGH: ALL REVEALED

This is the spoiler chapter, the one that gives away everything. It takes you step by step through the entire game, solving each puzzle and showing you exactly what to do to get from the beginning to the end, assuming no missed steps and virtual clairvoyance on the part of the player. At the end of the chapter, you will find brief descriptions of some of the alternate endings to the Riven saga.

"Walkthrough: All Revealed" will actually be most useful to you after completing the game, because it will help you piece together everything and see, in one package, how it all works and how you might have done things differently. Do not read this chapter if you want a chance to work things out for yourself!

Wherever you're coming from, you decide how much you want the writers of this book to tell you. Read the section above entitled "Vague to Specific: How Much Do You Want To Know?" to learn the four symbols representing the level of spoiler provided by each chapter.

If all you want is a general overview of the game mechanics—what the different cursors are and how to move around—read Chapter 2, "Roaming Through Riven." There are also some very general suggestions regarding gameplay, things to keep in mind as you move from to place to place.

You're stuck, but you don't want us to tell you the answer. If all you want are some gentle hints, check out Chapter 3, "The Islands of Riven: Hints and Musings." The hints are arranged by location, puzzle, or problem, top to bottom, vague to more specific and direct. You might want to use an index card to cover up the hints farther down each list, which will enable you to reveal each hint one at a time without giving away more than you want to know.

Even with all of our carefully worded hints, the twisted cunning of a particular puzzle or set of clues is just too much. What you want is straight talk about how to solve a particular problem, but without having the answer handed to you on a platter. If you want to see maps of the various locations, or would like a list of the puzzles and problems you must solve in each location, with some hints on how to go about it, go to Chapter 4, "The Islands of Riven: Maps and Specifics."

Okay, okay! Enough hints, vague suggestions, and cute stuff! If you read the words "Have you checked the entire room carefully for clues?" just one more time, you're going to commit cybercide! You're up against a steel-plated brick wall, and there is no way you're going to solve this puzzle in anything less than a decade or two.

If you want the specific solutions to each of Riven's puzzles, and step-by-step revelations of how each problem can be worked out, refer to Chapter 5, "Puzzles and Problems: The Solutions." If you would rather see a walkthrough that reveals everything, taking you from start to finish in the shortest possible time, read Chapter 6, "Walkthrough: All Revealed." This takes you through all of Riven using the most direct path possible, but be warned that you will lose most of the flavor and enjoyment of the game this way. Chapter 6 is best used after you've already successfully completed the game as a way of determining how well you did, or to see how else the game might have ended.

And finally, before you begin, here is one free piece of advice for playing Riven: Take your time! Enjoy, savor each location. Live it. Think about it. Turn it around in your mind. Take the time to puzzle each mystery out, rather than reaching for this book every time you face a problem that, at first glance, appears insoluble.

Riven is a universe of startling complexity, realism, consistency, and thoughtfulness. Some of the problems are extraordinarily difficult, but you can work them out if you think them through. There are no time limits, but there is a universe of satisfaction that comes with each successful solution, each mastered clue, each completed link.

Chapter Two

ROAMING THROUGH RIVEN

This is a Beetle chapter. It gives away very little in the way of game secrets or solutions.

Riven has a player interface that is simple, direct, and natural, almost as though you're physically in the world you are exploring. Getting around is literally a matter of pointing and clicking.

Notice the hand-shaped cursor on your screen. The appearance of the cursor changes depending on the actions that are available to you.

To Walk Forward

Move the pointing cursor to the spot on the path to which you want to go and click. The view on your screen subsequently changes to reflect your changed point of view. Sometimes you must click on a particular part of the screen to move forward. Note that there will also be times when it is simply not possible to move any farther. If clicking on the view ahead has no effect, turn left or right or try looking up or down to find another route.

To Take a Left or Right Path

As you approach an intersection, you can choose which path to take by moving the forward cursor over the desired path and clicking. With sharp turns, you may need to move abreast of the intersection, turn, and then move forward normally.

Turn Left/Right

Move the cursor to the left or right side of the screen, and watch it point in the indicated direction. Click, and your point of view rotates 90 degrees.

Turn Around

In the open, turn left or right twice to turn yourself around and face back the way you came. In close quarters—a cavern, say, or a tunnel—the left- or right-pointing finger appears crooked, as though pointing back over your shoulder. Clicking when you see this cursor will turn you 180 degrees.

Look Up/Move Up

Move the cursor to the top of the screen. If the up-pointing hand turns from palm away from you to palm facing you, so that you can see the fingers, clicking the mouse enables you to look or move in the direction in which the hand is pointing. Note that it is not always possible to look or move up.

Look Down/Move Down/Move Back

Move the cursor to the bottom of the screen. If the cursor changes to a down-pointing hand, clicking enables you to look down (over the edge of a cliff, for example), move down (descend a ladder), or move back (retreat from a close-up view). Note that these actions are not always possible.

PUSH/PICK UP/HANDLE/MANIPULATE

Keep an eye on your cursor. If there is something on your screen that can be manipulated—for example, a switch that can be thrown—the icon changes to an open hand. Click or click and drag to manipulate the object.

ZIP

When the Zip feature is selected in the menu bar, the cursor may change into a small lightning bolt when it is moved to a particular area of the landscape. If you see the lightning bolt, you can zip directly to that location. This is a great time saver when you have to do a lot of trekking back and forth. Just remember that there's a lot to be learned from the landscape—don't miss it all in the rush!

The world of Riven is there for you to explore. Experiment! Try everything! You will very soon find that the cursor controls are second nature. Just remember, if something doesn't work, try something else. There's got to be a way to get to where you're going!

GENERAL HINTS TO FOLLOW WHILE EXPLORING RIVEN

This is a hint book, so here are a few very general hints, things to keep in mind as you explore the complex, beautiful, and fascinating world called Riven.

EXAMINE EVERYTHING

There are numerous objects in Riven that allow you a closer look. Click on them to get a better view. Some devices enable you to further manipulate them—opening them or turning them on—and these may be important. Play with everything and note the results. Several devices have eyepieces, peepholes, or image viewing areas that require an up-close peek. Click on them to have a look.

HAVE A LOOK AROUND

The panoramas of the Riven sea- and landscapes are breathtakingly spectacular. Stop frequently and take a careful look around. Admire the scenery...but also, watch for geographical clues. Try to orient yourself in the landscape. Be especially aware of the various buildings and structures, and how they're sited on the various islands. You will want to pick up on such geographical clues as the location of certain bridges, where they lead to, whether they're open or closed, and so on.

IF IN DOUBT, TURN IT ON

Try everything, throw every switch, pull every lever, and note the results. While there are some mechanisms in Riven that must be set in a particular combination with other mechanisms, or which must be turned off so something else can be turned on, in general it's in your best interests to turn on everything.

UNDERSTAND THE MECHANISMS

You will encounter numerous mechanisms in Riven, strange devices that you must manipulate to open, move, look into, or turn on. Examine all such machines carefully by moving the cursor all over them, checking for those areas that seem to let you manipulate them in some way. Then click and drag on the various controls. Try different combinations. Try to understand what the thing does, and what it's used for. There may be subtle clues—a new sound or a change in some part of the landscape around you. Try to pick up on these clues and piece them together, forming a picture of how the machine works and why.

BE SYSTEMATIC

One lever may turn the power on or off for a number of locations, depending on how it is set. You may need to experiment by throwing the lever to one position, and then moving around and observing things to see what was turned on and what was turned off. Then you can return and try it in a different position.

BE OBSERVANT

Nothing in Riven was put there without a reason. Note such relatively minor details as where a steam pipe vanishes into the rock...and try to figure out where that same pipe emerges on the other side. Find out what it's connected to, and you might figure out what it's for! Be aware, too, of the sounds you hear. A few will be important enough that you will want to take note of them, so that you can remember them later.

BE PERSISTENT

Some puzzles may take many, many tries to crack. Some will require you to travel back and forth between widely separated parts of an island, or even between several different islands, before you've assembled all of the necessary clues. You may notice something new about a scene each time you go there. Keep at it!

READ THE JOURNALS

Atrus gives you his journal at the beginning of the game. Later, you may be able to acquire or read the journals kept by Catherine and Gehn. Read them! They are not there solely as background or atmosphere. There may be specific clues—even codes or the solutions to specific puzzles—hidden within these pages.

KEEP A NOTEBOOK

Don't trust your memory, especially if gameplay is going to extend over a period of weeks or months! In the course of your explorations, you will be required to learn certain symbols and relate those symbols to other things. When you see a symbol that is obviously intended as something more than decoration, copy it down. You will probably need it later!

MAKE MAPS

Veteran game players don't need this next piece of advice: Make maps of your journeys, and note what you find at different points along the way. Chapter 4 of this book includes maps of all of your destinations, but the thrill of discovery and the satisfaction of a deduction confirmed will be much richer if you keep that chapter closed for the time being, and draw your own maps as you explore. There are important clues in the relationships of certain structures, one with another, and the function of some controls can be inferred by noting the existence of pipe or walkway connections.

KEEP A JOURNAL

Atrus, Gehn, and Catherine all keep journals of their experiments, thoughts, and decisions. Shouldn't you? Some puzzle solutions require careful thought and the accumulation of clues from widely diverse locales. Many clues you acquire won't be needed until late in the game, when the larger picture finally begins to make sense. A journal of your thoughts and musings and speculations might help you pick up on subtle but necessary clues.

SAVE FREQUENTLY

Here's another piece of advice that veteran gamers recognize: Save often! You will have to do a lot of traveling to work out the various puzzles and problems; it would be a real shame if you were almost all the way through...and then discovered that you'd made a mistake or a rash assumption, and had to return to the beginning to retrace your steps! In general, save before traveling to another island or before getting too deeply involved in a new puzzle. That way, if things go wrong, you can restore your game from your last save, instead of repeating the whole thing.

TAKE YOUR TIME!

Riven is an extraordinarily rich and complex world. You are under no time restraints and you are not in a race. Take your time and enjoy the experience! It may take you many gaming sessions to crack a particular puzzle, numerous restores from saved games, and many different approaches to find the right sequence or code.

Chapter Three

THE ISLANDS OF RIVEN: HINTS AND MUSINGS

This chapter is designed to provide you with hints and clues to further your explorations of the world of Riven. It is divided into seven sections, five for the five islands of Riven, and two others for—well, call them "other places" for now. If you need help for a particular location or problem, find the appropriate section and look down through the headers until you find the list of clues you need.

The clues are arranged from top to bottom, more general to more specific, so you might want to use a piece of paper or an index card to cover up the clues lower on the list. That way, you will reveal only what you want revealed, and not see too much.

This section is rated as Frog. It gives away some of the mystery and will certainly make some of Riven's puzzles easier to figure out. It does not present specific solutions, however.

TEMPLE ISLAND

Temple Island is the place where you start your quest. There are a number of specific sites and machines located here, all of which will be important to the game.

THE OPENING DRAMA

When you arrive, you're trapped in a cage. A man in a dirty white uniform and carrying a knife or short sword in a scabbard appears, tries to talk to you in an unknown language, then grabs your Trap Book. A moment later, he slaps his neck as though stung, then collapses, the victim of a blow-gun dart. Next, another man appears, his face masked. He takes the book, operates the lever that opens your cage, and smashes the cage mechanism.

- ▶ Does all of this tell you anything about the people of Riven?

- ▶ The first man wears a uniform, though it looks more like it is wearing him.

- ▶ Does that tell you anything about a local government or power structure?

- ▶ He's attacked by someone who moves cautiously, a guerrilla or rebel. What does that tell you about Rivenese society?

THERE'S NOTHING YOU CAN DO AT THIS POINT ABOUT THE RIVENESE OR ABOUT GETTING YOUR TRAP BOOK BACK. STILL, YOU SHOULD TRY TO BE AWARE OF RIVENESE CULTURE AND LIFE. GEHN FANCIES HIMSELF TO BE THE CREATOR OF THIS WORLD AND ITS PEOPLE. COULD THERE POSSIBLY BE DISSENT HERE?

THE FIRST MECHANISM

When you are first released from the cage that imprisons you upon your arrival in Riven, you can see a mechanism of some sort—like a steel ice-cream cone—located just ahead.

▶ What might this be for?

▶ Carefully examine the structure and what it is built on.

▶ The controls don't work. You will have to go somewhere else to switch on the power.

▶ Does the pipe give you a hint as to where the power might come from?

▶ The device appears focused on a particular point. What is at that point?

▶ Obviously, you will need some sort of code to open the cover.

▶ What is that on the face of the machine. An eyepiece? It almost looks like the eyepiece for some kind of strange microscope or telescope...a viewing instrument of some kind, certainly.

TIP

THIS SHOULD WARN YOU THAT NOT EVERYTHING IN RIVEN IS POWERED WHEN YOU FIND IT. YOU'LL BE LOOKING FOR A NUMBER OF VALVES OR SWITCHES TO GET THINGS RUNNING AGAIN WHILE YOU'RE HERE.

THE GATE ROOM

Your first serious challenge upon arriving on Riven is the Gate Room, a five-sided chamber that rotates 72 degrees clockwise each time you press the button in the antechamber outside.

▶ Study the room, and try to understand the geometry. You might want to draw a map.

▶ There are only two doors inside the Gate Room, but they can align with any of five outer gateways in various combinations, leading in various directions.

▶ Looking through the peephole each time the gate is closed will give you clues to what is happening, and how the room is supposed to work.

▶ The room can access five different gateways. It can access only two of these at a time, because there are only two open doors within the revolving room.

▶ Call the door you first entered Position 1. The other gateways can be identified as Positions 2, 3, 4, and 5, going clockwise around the room.

▶ When you first enter the Gate Room, the open doors are at 1 and 3. Access to Position 3 is blocked by a metal grate, which must be opened elsewhere.

▶ By rotating the room three times, you can align the open doors with Positions 1 and 4. Again, a metal grate blocks access to the doorway at 4.

▶ To get at any of the doorways other than 1, 3, and 4, obviously, you will have to find another way into the Gate Room. Either you'll have to come at 3 or 4 from the other side, looking for a way to open them, or you must find a way to reach either 2 or 5.

▶ Explore. Try to visualize the layout of the room and its surroundings. Where might Position 2 be in relation to the outside of the hill? Where might Position 5 be?

▶ Is there anything to suggest an approach to one of those positions?

▶ When you find access to another Gate Position, you will be able to rotate the room so you can enter from that position.

▶ Keep this 1-2-3-4-5 geometry in mind as you experiment with rotating the room. To get to one position, you may have to rotate the room several times, go somewhere else, then rotate again to reach the desired configuration.

TIP

IN YOUR EXPLORATIONS, KEEP AN EYE OUT FOR SWITCHES, LEVERS, AND VALVES THAT MIGHT FURTHER YOUR QUEST. YOU'LL HAVE TO RAISE THOSE GRATES BLOCKING POSITIONS 3 AND 4 IN THE GATE ROOM, FOR ONE THING, AND YOU JUST MIGHT FIND SOME NECESSARY POWER CONTROLS!

THE GREAT GOLDEN DOME

This enormous dome looms high above Temple Island and appears to be an important site.

- ▶ Obviously, the way to reach the dome is through the Gate Room.

- ▶ You'll have to solve the Gate Room puzzle to enter the dome.

- ▶ Once you find the way through the Gate Room to Position 3, you can cross the bridge and enter the dome.

- ▶ Explore every catwalk you can reach. Find steam valves that you can turn. Try to determine what the steam pipes are connected to.

- ▶ Note the lever inside the entrance to the dome. The power is off. Can you find out how to turn it on?

- ▶ What does the lever do?

- ▶ Note the gap in the catwalk inside the dome.

- ▶ That large wheel could be the control to connect the catwalks, but you can't reach it from here.

- ▶ Obviously, there's a way into the Golden Dome from someplace else. Keep this in mind as you explore further.

 *TIP*

AS YOU CONTINUE YOUR EXPLORATIONS, TRY TO WORK OUT ROUGH MAPS OF WHAT YOU FIND. THE RELATIVE POSITIONS OF WHAT YOU SEE MAY HOLD IMPORTANT CLUES. THIS APPLIES TO OTHER ISLANDS YOU MIGHT SEE IN THE DISTANCE. IF YOU SEE A NEARBY ISLAND WITH BRIDGES OR OTHER STRUCTURES ON IT, TRY TO WORK OUT ITS POSITION RELATIVE TO THE ISLAND YOU'RE ON NOW.

THE FIRE MARBLE DOME

You may see one of these strange spinning domes on your first visit to Temple Island, but you won't be able to get at it yet. Keep your eye out for similar devices as you explore the islands of Riven.

THE TEMPLE AND ITS ENVIRONS

Across the bridge from the main entrance of the Gate Room is what at first looks like a separate island but is, in fact, a peninsula nearly sundered from the main island by the sea. Sooner or later, your explorations will take you here.

- ▶ Examine the passageway carefully as you go down.

- ▶ What's behind that door?

- ▶ Explore everything carefully. Push the buttons, pull the levers, and try to see what does what.

- ▶ When you've explored all that you can in the first room, follow the main passageway further. What do you find?

- ▶ If you find the big door in the main Temple closed, you will need to backtrack to find the control. Where might the room controls be?

- ▶ The large room at the end of the passageway is a Temple area. The smaller room higher up the passageway appears to be a projection room of some sort.

- ▶ Think of the "Great and Powerful Oz," and "that man behind the curtain." What does this set-up tell you about the guy who runs this place?

- ▶ The main doorway to the Temple leads to some kind of conveyance. Where might that take you?

TIP

KNOW YOUR ENEMY. GEHN CREATED THIS PLACE. KEEP AN EYE OUT FOR CLUES TO THE PSYCHOLOGY OF THE MAN, SO THAT YOU CAN TAKE HIS MEASURE.

After exploring the Gate Room, the Great Golden Dome, and the Temple Door, you are finished with Temple Island, at least for now.

JUNGLE ISLAND

A brief examination of the control panel of the mag-lev tram car outside the Temple door should suffice to show how it works. Operating the car will carry you on a wild and exciting ride across the ocean to neighboring Jungle Island.

EYES AND ANIMALS—THE FIRST SITE

When you first arrive on Jungle Island, explore carefully the area where the tram car docks.

- ▶ Can you find anything unusual near the tram?

- ▶ What does the eye shape do?

- ▶ Is there anything interesting or unusual about the eye?

- ▶ This is a tough one, and quite subjective. Go partway up the steps, turn, and look back. Can you see anything unusual about the mouth of the tunnel?

- ▶ Can you make out an animal shape, one with the wooden eye positioned in the place where a real eye would be?

 *TIP*

AS ALWAYS, NOTE EVERYTHING YOU SEE AND HEAR. THERE ARE CLUES YOU'LL NEED, OFTEN QUITE SUBTLE ONES, EVERYWHERE.

EYES AND ANIMALS—THE SECOND SITE

Follow the steps up, then down, and turn left at the T-intersection.

- ▶ Ahead, if you're observant...what do you see?

- ▶ They're alive. Each time you move, they raise their heads, as if disturbed.

▶ You can leave the path and try to get closer. Can you sneak up on them without scaring them?

▶ How close can you get?

▶ If you move while their heads are up, you will frighten them off.

▶ Try to get close enough to hear one of them deliver a sharp, harsh bark.

▶ Explore the rest of the beach area. Is there anything else of interest?

▶ Can you find another painted, wooden eye?

▶ Is the eye associated with another animal-like shape of some kind?

▶ What is unusual about this eye? Make a note of what you see and hear.

 *TIP*

THINK ABOUT IT. WHO'S BEEN LEAVING THESE WOODEN EYES ALL OVER THE PLACE, WITH THE CRYPTIC SILHOUETTES? GEHN? THAT HARDLY SEEMS LIKELY. REMEMBER THE ATTACK YOU WITNESSED WHEN YOU FIRST ARRIVED ON RIVEN. COULD SOME COVERT OR SECRET GROUP BE AT WORK HERE?

EYES AND ANIMALS—THE THIRD SITE

Go back to the point where you left the path, then turn left. Follow the path through the side of a mountain, and emerge overlooking Village Lake.

▶ Explore the raised platform and ladders carefully. Do you see anything unusual?

▶ You should see what looks like a stone pool with an irregular bottom.

▶ Turn the petcock to the right. The water will create the silhouette of something, although it may be difficult to make out exactly what.

▶ Can you find another wooden eye?

▶ Make a note of what you see on the eye, what you hear when you turn it, and the shape of the silhouette revealed in the stone pool.

AND... WHILE YOU'RE HERE, HAVE A GOOD LOOK AROUND AND SEE IF YOU CAN TELL WHAT YOUR NEXT OBJECTIVE SHOULD BE.

THE SUBMARINE

From the stone pool, you can look up and to the left and make out a strange, spherical craft made of iron on a ledge high overhead. When you stare down into the shimmering waters of Village Lake, you can just make out what might be iron rails crossing the lake's bottom. Is there a connection?

▶ Is that another ladder on the far side of the pool? Where does it lead?

▶ You've gone as far as you can at this end of the path. But remember this place. You might have use for it later.

▶ You're going to have to find another way to reach the submarine.

▶ Follow the path back the way you came...past the lagoon where you saw the Sunners basking on a rock, up the hill and over the top, across the rope bridge. Make your way to the wooden pier/walkway that you saw from the other side of Village Lake. Ahead, you should be able to see the village.

▶ From the stone pool at the other end of the path you could see the village beyond the submarine. Can you work out the relative positions of where you were and where the sub is now?

- At some point, you will need to start climbing ladders and crossing plank bridges. Eventually you will reach the submarine, resting on a ledge at what seems to be some sort of ceremonial center.

- There's a lever. What does it do?

- How can you reach the submarine now?

- You will have to retrace your steps again, all the way back and around, past the Sunner rock, past the stone pool, and down the ladders, where you will find that the submarine is now waiting at the bottom of a hole in the water.

TIP

UNLESS YOU START CONSULTING CHAPTER 6 IN THIS BOOK REGULARLY, YOU'RE GOING TO BE DOING A LOT OF BACKTRACKING HERE! DON'T WORRY. THAT'S PART OF THE FUN, AND A WAY OF BECOMING VERY FAMILIAR WITH THIS WORLD. DON'T LET FAMILIARITY BLIND YOU, THOUGH, TO THINGS YOU MIGHT NOT HAVE NOTICED YOUR FIRST TIME THROUGH!

THE SUBMARINE CIRCUIT

It's not hard to decipher how the submarine works. You will have to do some mapping, though, to figure out where the lake-bottom tracks take you, and how to get where you want to go.

- Can you relate the directions of the branching tracks with the layout of docks and piers you've seen so far on the surface?

- Can you get at all of the docks?

- Without a ladder from the docks, you're stuck inside the sub.

- Perhaps you need to find a control room of some sort.

▶ When you find the Control Room, two switches are up, three are down.

▶ Can you correlate that with the number of ladders you've seen up or down?

▶ What happens when you have all of the switches thrown?

MAPS WILL HELP WITH THIS ONE, ESPECIALLY IF YOU CAN LINK UP WHAT YOU SEE ON THE SURFACE WITH THE PROBABLE DIRECTIONS OF THE UNDER-WATER RAILS.

THE SCHOOL ROOM

This seems to be where the Rivenese children are taught their letters and numbers. You might learn something useful here.

▶ Do any of the artifacts found in the schoolroom tell you anything about Gehn's character, or about the life of the people living under his rule?

▶ What do you think the point of the Wahrk Hangman Toy is? Besides instilling psychological terror in children, that is.

▶ Play the game and study the symbols.

▶ Is there a relationship with symbols you've seen elsewhere?

RIVENESE MATHEMATICS USES A BASE 5 NUMBERING SYSTEM. TRY TO LEARN ALL OF THE NUMBERS BETWEEN 1 AND 10, AND FIGURE OUT HOW THE SERIES OF 6 THROUGH 10 IS BUILT ON 1 THROUGH 5.

THE JUNGLE ISLAND FIRE MARBLE DOME

Just figuring out how to get to the dome is a problem, although you can see it turning atop its pedestal of rock near the sullen glow of a magma-filled fissure.

▶ What structure is located near the dome?

▶ Might that have anything to do with reaching the dome?

▶ Actually, there are two ways to reach it. If you don't find the path during your first exploration of the island, you should be able to find a back way in later.

 *TIP*

ONCE YOU FIND YOUR WAY TO THE DOME, BE SURE TO RECORD THE SYMBOL THAT OPENS IT IN THE KINETOSCOPE.

TAKE NOTE OF WHAT THE FIRE MARBLE DOME IS BUILT ON. YOU'LL NEED TO REMEMBER THAT LATER.

GEHN'S ELEVATED THRONE

If you find your way to the Jungle Island Fire Marble Dome, you'll be able to reach this building, perched on a cliff high above Village Lake. Figuring out what the levers do is easy enough. Now that you're here, what should you do?

▶ The throne looks almost directly down on the Wahrk Gallows, a place of execution. This place must have something to do with the gallows and what happens there.

▶ Have you tried reaching the Wahrk Gallows from the submarine yet?

▶ Were you able to get to the center of the gallows platform? Why not?

▶ Is there any reason to think you might want to explore in that direction?

▶ Does one of the levers by the throne solve your problem?

 *TIP*

REMEMBER THE INJUNCTION TO THROW EVERY LEVER, AND TRY EVERY CONTROL.

THE FOURTH EYE

Finding three of the wooden eyes on Jungle Island is relatively easy, especially if you have this book in hand. The fourth eye is a bit tougher.

▶ Have you searched all of the island thoroughly?

▶ Do you remember how you went off the trail a bit, back by Sunner Rock?

▶ Might there be other places where you can leave the path?

▶ Have you attached any significance, as yet, to the giant metal daggers that are scattered about Riven?

▶ Those daggers were not left there by Gehn.

▶ The daggers are associated with someone fighting against Gehn...someone leaving subtle clues to something else.

▶ Try searching the paths in the jungle. Watch for places where you can leave the path.

THE FOURTH EYE DOES NOT HAVE AN ANIMAL SHAPE ASSOCIATED WITH IT, AS THE FIRST THREE DID. CAN YOU IDENTIFY THE ANIMAL THIS EYE IS ASSOCIATED WITH FROM THE SOUND IT MAKES?

THINK ABOUT IT. ONE NUMBER HAS BEEN FIGURING LARGE IN YOUR DISCOVERIES SO FAR. WHAT IS IT? HOW MANY WOODEN EYES—AND THE ANIMALS ASSOCIATED WITH THEM—MIGHT THERE BE ALL TOGETHER

You are done with Jungle Island when you've found the wooden eyes and associated each with an animal and with a symbol, when you've learned what the symbols mean, when you've found out how to reach the Fire Marble Dome, entered Gehn's Throne Tower, learned the secret of the Wahrk Gallows, and discovered a new gateway. It may require several visits to the island to uncover all of this. Keep at it!

CRATER ISLAND

You have several options for getting off Jungle Island, but we'll assume that you find the logging-car ride from the clear-cut area near the jungle. This leads you, in wild and surrealistic fashion, along an underwater path to a neighboring island, Crater Island. In fact, you may have discovered this route by accident early in your explorations of Jungle Island, since all you need to do is follow a path to a tunnel, climb down, and push a lever.

THE CENTRAL POWER VALVE

Nothing works until you switch the power valve you'll find out in the middle of the lake.

- ▶ How many pipes are there?

- ▶ One pipe is different from the others and seems to provide power to those facilities along the cliff in the distance all of the time.

- ▶ Three of the pipes go to different places and are powered in turn by moving the steam valve lever.

- ▶ Where do the three pipes lead?

EXPERIMENT. POWER UP ONE MACHINE, THEN GO CHECK OUT THE RESULTS.

THE BOILER PUZZLE

Though you arrive on a log chipper, the first structure you see on this island is a huge boiler, which reduces log chips to a kind of paste for making paper. You must figure out how it works to get anywhere on this island.

- ▶ Explore the beach as far as you can in all directions. Looks like a dead end, doesn't it?

- ▶ Is there anything about the boiler that suggests another exit?

▶ Can you get inside the boiler?

▶ Experiment with the controls. One valve powers alternately the mechanism for filling and emptying the tank with water, and the control for raising and lowering a grate inside the tank.

▶ Is the furnace on? Can you turn it off?

▶ Can you find a combination of settings that lets you get inside the tank?

▶ Can you reach the central tube and ladder?

▶ What happens when you raise the grate?

IN ORDER FOR YOU TO WALK ACROSS TO THE LADDER INSIDE THE TANK AND GO DOWN THE LADDER, THE GRATE NEEDS TO BE RAISED, THE TANK EMPTIED OF WATER, AND THE FURNACE TURNED OFF.

THE TUNNEL TAKES YOU ON A LONG, DARK CRAWL, FOLLOWED BY A LONG CLIMB UP A LADDER, AND DEPOSITS YOU FROM A DRAINAGE PIPE HIGH UP ON THE MOUNTAIN. FROM THERE, YOU'LL NEED TO FIND A PATH LEADING OVER THE CREST AND DOWN TO A RAILED PLATFORM.

CATCHING FROGS

You reach the railed balcony and find the locked hatch that opens to the ladder going back down to the beach. At least you won't have to crawl back through that drainage pipe if you need to go back to the power control in the lake again! Now go through the double doors in the face of the cliff.

▶ Can you figure out how to work the trap apparatus?

▶ It's pretty easy. The spherical device that opens from the top is a trap. The tiny pellets to the right are food.

▶ Depending on where you left the power setting in the lake, you may need to go back and restore power to this facility.

- ▶ Try to catch a frog. Listen to its call.

- ▶ Match the frog's call in your mind with the eye you found on Jungle Island, the one inside the frog silhouette in the rocks. Now, why do you think Gehn might be trapping frogs?

- ▶ On your way back to the double doors...did you miss anything?

- ▶ There are other passageways here. Can you find them?

- ▶ Try closing the doors.

YOU MAY HAVE SEEN THIS PSYCHOLOGY OF DOOR-DESIGN IN ACTION BEFORE...DOORS THAT, WHEN THEY OPEN, SEAL OFF ANOTHER DOOR. VERY ECONOMICAL IN TERMS OF MOTION. VERY SNEAKY...

THE CRATER ISLAND FIRE MARBLE DOME

Down the stairs to your left as you face the front doors is the chamber where the Fire Marble Dome for this island is hidden. This may be the first Fire Marble Dome you've been able to get close to.

- ▶ The dome is spinning rapidly. Do you notice anything interesting about the dome, something engraved on the surface?

- ▶ You don't see any controls. Where might they be hidden?

- ▶ Watch it! The architect is pulling the same trick on you he pulled before!

- ▶ The device in the hidden cave is a kinetoscope, a mechanism that can pick up separate images through a rotating shutter as they turn past the lens, allowing them to be viewed as a kind of motion picture.

- ▶ The push button on top of the device catches one "frame" of the movie, one of the passing symbols.

- ▶ Is there anything about the rotating symbols suggesting that one symbol is more important than the others?

▶ Can you click the button on the kinetoscope in order to catch that one, highlighted symbol?

▶ You got it! The dome is open. Inside is a dazzling, burnished, golden sphere—a giant, fiery marble, in fact. Can you make out what's inside the Fire Marble through the glass port?

▶ What is the mechanism of sliders and button for? How does it work?

▶ You will need another code to operate this device.

▶ Where might such a code be found? Who constructed the dome, and for what possible purpose?

DON'T FORGET TO MAKE A NOTE OF THE SYMBOL THAT OPENED THE DOME. YOU MIGHT NEED IT LATER.

WHILE YOU'RE IN THE FIRE MARBLE DOME CHAMBER ON CRATER ISLAND, LOOK UP. SEE THAT HOLE IN THE CEILING, LIKE A CRATER MOUTH? REMEMBER THAT. THE INFORMATION WILL BE USEFUL LATER.

GEHN'S LABORATORY

The front door to the lab is locked, as you'll find if you follow the path through the hidden door to the right of the double doors. How else might you get in?

▶ Explore the path revealed to the right of the double doors as you go out.

▶ Can you get into Gehn's lab this way?

▶ As you were on the walkway, did you hear a sound you've heard before? What did it sound like?

▶ What happens to the sound when you throw the lever?

▶ What have you just done?

▶ After throwing the lever, check the frog-trap station again. Anything different?

▶ Can you climb up into the ventilator shaft?

▶ Where does that take you?

You are finished with Crater Island when you have traveled through the boiler to the double doors, solved the problem of the frog-catching apparatus, the fan, and the fan motor switch so that you can reach Gehn's laboratory, found the Fire Marble Dome, and followed the path past the lab to lower the drawbridge between Crater Island and the Great Golden Dome.

ONCE YOU'RE IN THE LAB, TAKE YOUR TIME AND CHECK IT OUT CAREFULLY. THERE'S A LOT TO BE FOUND HERE, INCLUDING SOME INFORMATION VITAL FOR THE SUCCESSFUL COMPLETION OF YOUR QUEST.

ONCE YOU REACH THE GOLDEN DOME FROM CRATER ISLAND, YOU MAY WANT TO GO ON THROUGH AND TO THE LEFT TO THE PLACE WHERE AN EXTENSION OF THE CATWALK HAS BEEN DRAWN BACK. TURN THE WHEEL TO COMPLETE THE CATWALK AND OPEN THE PATH ALL THE WAY BACK TO THE GATE ROOM.

AND, WHILE YOU'RE AT IT, YOU MIGHT WANT TO PULL THE LEVER THAT RAISES THE BRIDGE FROM THE GATE ROOM TO A POINT SOMEWHERE ABOVE YOUR HEAD IN THE GOLDEN DOME. DOING SO NOW WILL SAVE YOU SOME DETOURS LATER ON.

AND FINALLY, NOW IS YOUR CHANCE TO FOLLOW THE CATWALK OUTSIDE THE DOME AROUND TO POSITION 4 OF THE GATE ROOM, THROWING THE SWITCH TO OPEN THE DOOR THAT HAD YOU BLOCKED FROM THE OTHER SIDE.

You should now have three possible destinations. You can ride the logging car back to Jungle Island (by climbing the ladder near the chipper). You can follow the path past Gehn's lab back to the Golden Dome. (If, back when you were on Temple

Island before, you turned the lever to power up the western drawbridge, you should be able to operate it now when you reach the control lever.) Or you can take a mag-lev tram to a new island. We'll assume for now that you do the latter.

PLATEAU ISLAND

This is where you collect some serious clues to the major puzzles that you'll need to solve to reach the end of your quest. Here you'll start putting it all together.

THE PLATEAU MAP

If you've been paying attention, you'll recognize this as a map of Riven.

- ▶ Push each shape on the panel on the railing.

- ▶ What happens to the corresponding island?

- ▶ Can you correlate the islands on the Plateau Map with the island shapes on the control?

- ▶ What happens when you press each island symbol on the control panel? There are some seriously twisted physics going on here!

 *TIP*

DID YOU REALIZE THAT THERE ARE FIVE RIVENESE ISLANDS IN ALL? THERE HAVE BEEN CLUES TO THIS FACT BEFORE (THE MAP/SIGN ON THE RAILING INSIDE THE FIRST DOOR YOU ENTERED IN THE GREAT GOLDEN DOME, FOR ONE) BUT THIS IS THE FIRST TIME YOU'VE HAD IT ALL LAID OUT FOR YOU.

THE MAP ROOM PUZZLE

Obviously, you're supposed to learn something here, although exactly what it is might have you scratching your head for a long time. It's clear that the plateau-maps relate to these grid-maps of Riven's five islands, and that clicking on each square brings up a 3D relief map of that region. But why? What are you supposed to do with this?

▶ At first you might not even be able to reach the Map Room. Have you checked the position overlooking the Plateau Map yet?

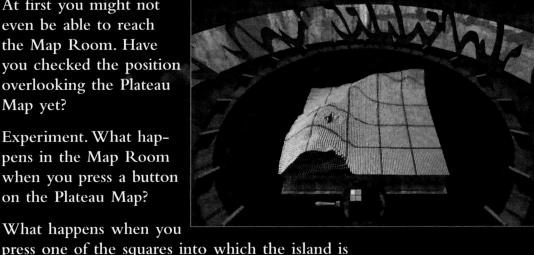

▶ Experiment. What happens in the Map Room when you press a button on the Plateau Map?

▶ What happens when you press one of the squares into which the island is divided?

▶ The creator of Riven did nothing without a purpose. There must have been something he was mapping on each of the five islands.

▶ What is the one specific significant artifact or construct that, so far, at least, has been common to every island you've visited?

▶ Might there be a reason for mapping all such features of the islands?

▶ You need to work out the map coordinates for each island map for the one feature common to all of the islands.

▶ The 3D relief images are divided into five-by-five grids but are not otherwise identified. You will have to either draw maps of your own, or invent your own grid system—something simple like A, B, C, D, and E across the top, and 1, 2, 3, 4, and 5 down the side. This would allow you, for example, to record the lower right square as "E-5."

▶ You will have to examine each map segment carefully, sometimes from different angles, to ascertain the right square.

▶ A clue to what you're looking for can be found if you consider the terrain near the Fire Marble Domes on Jungle Island, on Crater Island, and here on Plateau Island.

- On Plateau Island, the Fire Marble Dome rests just beyond a sharp, vertical cleft in the rock wall surrounding the lake.

- On Crater Island, the Fire Marble Dome was underground...but positioned directly under a crater or gap in the rock ceiling, open to the sky.

- These geographical features should let you locate the positions of the Fire Marble Domes on these three islands with accuracy.

BE VERY SURE TO COPY THE MAPS WITH THE DOME LOCATIONS, OR RECORD THE COORDINATES. YOU WILL NEED THEM LATER!

THE LAKE AND THE FIRE MARBLE DOME

The Map Room rests in the center of a crater lake. Another Fire Marble Dome can be seen turning beyond a cleft in the rocks. There are some clues here that you will need to figure out the Color Puzzle.

- What can you see in the lake, besides the Map Room building?

- How many of them are there?

- Can you distinguish different colors?

- The kinetoscope is broken, knocked out of alignment with the dome. It cannot be fixed.

- Can you stop the dome anyway?

- The problem of the broken kinetoscope can only be solved by a kind of brute force method.

To stop the dome rotation, you'll have to click the button on top of the kinetoscope rapidly—basically click the mouse as fast as you can—and try to catch the right symbol at random. This actually works for any of the Fire Marble Dome kinetoscopes if you have trouble catching the one correct symbol as it goes past.

Because the kinetoscope is broken, you will not be able to see the Fire Marble Dome's symbol through it. You'll have to look closely at the dome while it is still closed and spinning (if you've already opened it, you will have to close it again to do this) and see if you can identify the one yellow symbol...or at least narrow down the possibilities.

THE UNDERWATER VIEWING CHAMBER

You may have to think for a moment about how to get from one side of the mag-lev tram car chamber to the other. Obviously it must be possible to get over there; you can see a door on that side from the tram's cabin. But how to do it?

- ▶ The solution is obvious if you turn it around in your mind.

- ▶ Once you get over there, you'll go down a long, orange-lit corridor. At some point, you'll see someone—one of Gehn's scribes—who will dash off into a side chamber as soon as he sees you. Follow him, and you'll arrive in time to see him getting into another tram car at a different station and whooshing off. You won't be able to catch him...but remember this station for later.

- ▶ Keep following the main passageway, then to Gehn's Viewing Chamber.

- The device on the right has symbols on the dial. Do you recognize any of those symbols?

- What might the symbols refer to?

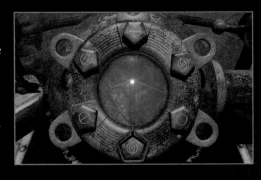

- Can you correlate the symbols with the color of the light showing in the display?

- The colored lights that switch on when you press the button match the colors painted on the wahrk totems you saw on the surface of the lake.

- You are looking for five colors, matched with five symbols. Unfortunately, there are six symbols in all, and—worse—one of the totems is missing and the light does not work.

FUN WITH WAHRKS: THE RED LIGHT APPAR-ENTLY CALLS A WAHRK IN CLOSE FOR FEEDING. TRY SWITCHING ON THE RED LIGHT, THEN LOOK UP, AND WATCH THE WAHRK APPROACH. IF YOU WANT TO MESS WITH THE WAHRK'S MIND, CALL HIM SEVERAL TIMES; EACH TIME YOU TURN ON THE LIGHT AND NO FOOD APPEARS, HE GETS TESTIER. THE FOURTH TIME HE SHOWS UP, HE GETS DOWNRIGHT NASTY...THEN WILL NOT RETURN AGAIN UNTIL MUCH LATER.

GEHN'S VIEWING CHAMBER: THE VIEWING SCREEN

- The left-hand wheel has two buttons, which appear to show views from two different cameras. What do they appear to show?

- One shows a woman, alone in a room somewhere. Who might she be?

- Both Atrus's and Gehn's journals mention a woman. Where might she be?

▶ The other button shows several views of Village Lake on Jungle Island.

▶ The views on Jungle Island seem to be coming from the small island in the middle of the lake with what looked like a lens or camera on it.

▶ Do any of the images appear unusual?

▶ One image appears to be a silhouette of sorts.

▶ Have you been looking for a fifth animal silhouette?

▶ Can you spot something like an eye, tiny and indistinct, within the silhouette's outline?

YOU CANNOT REACH THE WOODEN EYE REVEALED IN THIS VIEW. KNOWING THE IMPORTANCE OF THE NUMBER FIVE, HOWEVER, YOU SHOULD BE ABLE TO GUESS WHAT NUMBER-SYMBOL IS CARVED ON THE BACK OF THAT EYE. YOU NOW HAVE THE INFORMATION YOU NEED TO SOLVE THE PUZZLE OF THE TWENTY-FIVE STONES.

You are done with Plateau Island when you have figured out the Map Room Puzzle, found the Viewing Chamber, linked the various Fire Marble Dome symbols with specific colors, and noted the fifth animal silhouette.

You can now travel by tram either back to Crater Island, or, following the scribe, on to Jungle Island. If you have not previously solved the problem of the Wahrk Idol, reached the Jungle Island Fire Marble Dome, and gone on to find Gehn's Throne tower, now is your chance.

You'll probably want to go to Jungle Island, because by now you should have all the information you need to crack the puzzle of the Twenty-Five Stones...and reach the Age of the Rebel Moiety.

THE REBEL MOIETY AGE

FINDING THE REBEL WORLD

This may be one of the two or three most difficult problems in the game, but you must find your way here to successfully complete the game.

THE NATURE OF THE MOIETY

At one point or another, you are going to have to find a group of natives who call themselves "The Moiety." Who are they? How do you go about doing this?

> ▶ In your explorations so far, have you seen signs of discontent in the local population? Of fear? Of rebellion?

> ▶ Have you noticed clues that might tell you something about the nature of Gehn's rule over the Rivenese?

> ▶ The Moiety is what a band of rebels on Riven call themselves. What or who might they be rebelling against?

> ▶ The Moiety must have a safe haven from which they can carry out their operations in the world of Riven. Is that haven likely to be on one of the islands?

> ▶ The Moiety must operate virtually under the nose of Gehn, the architect and ruler of this world. How might they communicate with one another and with the natives whom they are trying to free?

> ▶ They are going to leave extremely subtle clues to teach the natives how to reach them, clues that Gehn might overlook.

SHAPES, SOUNDS, AND SYMBOLS

Someone has gone to a lot of trouble to place subtle clues to something important in various locations of one particular island. These clues involve distinctive shapes, specific sounds, and certain cryptic symbols.

> ▶ Is there a persistent artifact that has turned up several times in your explorations? Something that appears connected to a larger mystery?

▶ There are several locations on Jungle Island where a wooden artifact is found.

▶ Each artifact is painted like an eye.

▶ Each wooden eye makes a distinctive noise when it is turned

▶ The noise of each eye is different from the noise made by the others.

▶ Each wooden eye has a different symbol on the back. Can you determine what these symbols represent?

▶ This can be extraordinarily subtle, but some of the eyes are associated with a shape, a different shape for each eye. Can you spot the shapes and guess what they might represent?

▶ Does the sound the eye made relate in any way to the shapes?

▶ One wooden eye has no shape associated with it, but it makes a noise that you may have heard during your explorations. Can you identify the animal by hearing its call?

▶ The shapes in question are the shapes of animals.

▶ The wooden eyes sometimes appear in the relative positions of the actual eyes of the real animals.

▶ The sounds the wooden eyes make are the sounds made by those animals.

▶ Eventually, you should have a list of four animals, each identified by the sound it makes, each associated with a different symbol.

▶ Remember, you may not have the complete list.

▶ There is a fifth animal shape. You will need to look elsewhere to see it.

figured out what the symbols mean, you will still need one more piece to the puzzle—the fifth animal shape.

▶ You will have to search far and wide to spot this one.

▶ Be alert in your travels for a particular viewing perspective that seems to show an unusual or distinctive shape.

▶ You can identify the shape by looking for the eye. If there's something like a wooden eye in the appropriate place on something that might be an animal shape, that is one of the puzzle pieces to the Moiety World.

▶ You need to know the shape of the fifth animal. You do not need to actually reach the eye, as you do with the others.

▶ In fact, you can't reach the wooden eye on this one. You can only see it, from one particular vantage point.

▶ That vantage point is not on Jungle Island.

▶ The shape you're looking for, however, is on Jungle Island.

▶ There is no sound associated with this shape.

▶ You do not need to see the symbol on the back of the wooden eye associated with this shape...and a good thing, too, since you can't reach it. Once you identify the shape and put it together with the information you've already acquired, the identity of the necessary symbol will be more or less obvious.

FINDING THE MOIETY GATEWAY

Once you have the code—a list of animals and symbols that should tell you how to use them— you must still figure out where to use it.

▶ Again, have you learned anything during your explorations that might tell you what Gehn's rule is like in Riven?

- Are the people happy under that rule? Are they afraid?

- The Moiety has been fighting against Gehn. What might his response be to their rebellion?

- Are there clues anywhere about that might suggest how Gehn treats rebels he manages to capture?

- Investigate Village Lake on Jungle Island. One distinctive structure appears designed to eliminate rebels in a spectacular fashion.

- Call this device the Wahrk Gallows. Can you approach it? Can you use it to reach someplace else?

- Investigating the School Room will confirm how rebels are executed.

- Can you find the place where rebel prisoners might be held while they await their fate?

- The prisoner! He's gone!

- You were looking at the prison door when you turned the button. Where did he go? Not out the front door.

- Okay. If a rebel group is operating on the island, might they have worked out a means of rescuing those of their number who have fallen into Gehn's hands?

- Perhaps the prison cell requires a closer examination.

- Okay. That opens, but nothing else happens. Why? Is there anything more to be learned here? Check everything!

- Once you find the secret door, things will get very dark. Keep moving ahead. You'll come to some light eventually.

- Okay. Dead end. But...is there anything here that might cast some light on this situation?

- Back up the tunnel. Check carefully. Is there anything you might have missed seeing in the dark?

TIP

NO, THE GAME HASN'T DIED. IF YOUR SCREEN GOES COMPLETELY BLACK, IT'S JUST BECAUSE YOU'RE IN A PITCH-BLACK TUNNEL. KEEP MOVING FORWARD!

USING THE GATEWAY

Congratulations! You've found a strange, well-hidden room with even stranger decor. The dagger symbol on the far wall is covered by water somehow forced to obey some very different laws of physics from those you're used to. Might this be the gate you've been looking for?

▶ Examine the room. How many stones are there? What is on the stones?

▶ Have you seen any of these shapes before?

▶ Do these shapes relate to the animal shapes you've seen already?

▶ How many shapes have you discovered?

▶ Have you learned yet what the symbols associated with each shape represent? Does this suggest how to use the shapes?

▶ Try touching the stones. Obviously, they must be touched in a particular order.

▶ What is that order?

▶ Do you have all of the shapes you need?

▶ There are twenty-five shapes in all. What number has figured prominently in Riven thus far?

▶ This is the Fifth Age, there were five sides to the Gate Room, five arms to the star symbol, five beetles on the five pillars, and five islands.

▶ You need five animals shapes, entered in a particular order.

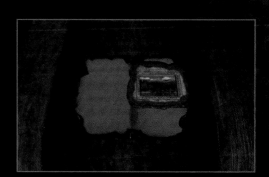

▶ You can solve the puzzle by brute force, trying different combinations in turn, but it will take a long time and be inordinately tedious.

▶ You can also leave this for later if you have not acquired all of the shapes yet.

 *TIP*

THREE OF THE SHAPES YOU ARE LOOKING FOR ARE RELATIVELY STRAIGHTFORWARD. ONE SHAPE MUST BE INFERRED BY THE SOUND MADE BY THE WOODEN EYE, BECAUSE THERE IS NO SHAPE AT THAT SITE. THE FIFTH SHAPE IS DIABOLICALLY SUBTLE AND CANNOT BE REACHED PHYSICALLY. YOU CAN SEE IT, HOWEVER, FROM ONE—AND ONLY ONE— SPOT ON ONE OF THE ISLANDS.

IN THE REBEL WORLD

Okay. Now that you're in the Rebel world, what do you do now?

- ▶ Explore your surroundings. Where are you?

- ▶ At some point in your explorations, a young woman enters your room. You can't understand her language, but she certainly seems to want to communicate something important.

- ▶ Listen closely to her speech. Did you hear a name you recognized?

- ▶ What does she give you?

- ▶ What does she seem to want you to do?

- ▶ You're obviously not going anywhere for a while. Maybe you should do what she says.

- ▶ After a time, the woman returns with something else. What does it look like?

- ▶ What do you see in the image in the book?

- ▶ Might this be the way back?

Once you have the journal and the Trap Book in your possession, you're ready to return to Jungle Island via the linking book the woman lays open on the table.

 *TIP*

WHAT THE WOMAN GAVE YOU IS IMPORTANT TO THE SUCCESSFUL COMPLETION OF THE GAME.

GEHN'S WORLD

REACHING GEHN'S WORLD

Finding out how to reach Gehn's world is probably the single most difficult problem to master.
The clues are subtle, the components of the puzzle obscure and widely scattered. Good luck!

THE LINKING BOOKS

▶ Travel between different Ages—the various created worlds—is accomplished
through special books.

▶ Have you seen any books yet during your travels,
other than the journals or the Trap Book, that is?

▶ Such books would be very well protected.

▶ Such books require a very great deal of power to activate them.

▶ Such books could be expected to be located in conve-
nient places all over Riven—where Gehn could reach
them quickly if he needed to—but in a place that
would keep the natives out.

▶ When you managed to open each of the Fire Marble
Domes so far, could you see anything through the
small glass window?

▶ Something like a book?

▶ The Fire Marble Domes are repositories for books
that link to Gehn's private hideaway.

*YOU ONLY NEED TO OPEN ONE OF THE FIRE
MARBLE DOMES TO ACCESS A LINKING BOOK. THE
ONLY REASON TO TRY OPENING ALL OF THE FIRE
MARBLE DOMES IS SO THAT YOU CAN IDENTIFY THE
CODE SYMBOL OF EACH ONE, AND LATER CORRELATE
THAT CODE SYMBOL WITH A PARTICULAR COLOR—
LEARNED DURING YOUR INVESTIGATIONS OF THE
COLOR WHEEL IN GEHN'S VIEWING CHAMBER
BENEATH PLATEAU ISLAND.*

you are still faced with a lock—five vertical sliders that must be moved along a horizontal scale to specific positions. Learning what those positions are is one of the major puzzles of the game.

- ▶ The horizontal scale looks like a ruler, laid out in five groups of five.

- ▶ The domes were built by Gehn. Where might he have left a note for himself, a reminder of the combination?

- ▶ By now, you should have learned the first ten numerals of the Rivenese numbering system.

- ▶ By now, too, you should have seen Gehn's lab journal and searched through it carefully.

- ▶ Is there anything in Gehn's lab journal that looks like a string of several numbers?

- ▶ Might that be the code?

- ▶ The slider scale allows you to enter numbers as high as 25. Unfortunately, you only know the first ten numbers.

- ▶ Some of the numbers in Gehn's journal may be higher than ten.

- ▶ Can you take what you know of the Rivenese numbering system and extrapolate what the rest of the numbers look like—enough, at least, for you to take a guess at what the numbers in the journal are?

RIVENESE NUMERALS—DERIVED FROM THE COUNTING SYSTEM OF LOST D'NI—ARE BASE FIVE. INSTEAD OF COUNTING BY TENS, A RIVENESE WOULD COUNT BY FIVES. "FIVE" IS WRITTEN AS A ONE ROTATED 90 DEGREES COUNTERCLOCKWISE; "TEN" IS A ROTATED TWO, "FIFTEEN" IS A ROTATED THREE, AND "TWENTY" IS A ROTATED FOUR. OTHER NUMERALS ARE CREATED BY COMBINING SYMBOLS. "EIGHT" IS A COMBINATION OF THE SYMBOLS FOR FIVE AND THREE. "SIXTEEN" IS FIFTEEN AND ONE. THE ONLY WILDCARD IN THE SERIES IS "25," WHICH LOOKS LIKE AN "X" IN A BOX. FORTUNATELY, YOU WON'T HAVE TO FIGURE OUT NUMBERS HIGHER THAN 25!

Once you think you have the sequence, move each slider to the appropriate position on the scale and press the button. If you've worked out the numbers correctly, the inner portion of the dome will open, and you will have access to the linking book.

Unfortunately, you're still not home free. The book is open, but it needs power—a very great deal of power—to work. Power to all of the Fire Marble Dome linking books in Riven comes from one place, and you will have to solve a final puzzle to figure out how to turn on the power.

FINDING THE FIRE MARBLE PUZZLE

There is one trek you yet must make in order to power up all of the Fire Marble Domes on Riven.

▶ What facility have you seen thus far in your travels that might conceivably provide a great deal of power to the Fire Marble Domes on all of the Riven islands?

▶ Is there a part of that facility you have not yet explored?

▶ You will need to raise a drawbridge from inside the facility. If you did this when you reached the Golden Dome from Crater Island earlier, then the way is open to the upper level of the dome from the Gate Room on Temple Island.

*YOU WON'T BE READY TO SOLVE THIS FINAL PUZ-
ZLE UNLESS YOU KNOW (OR CAN GUESS) WHAT
COLORS ARE ASSOCIATED WITH THE DIFFERENT
FIRE MARBLE DOMES, AND KNOW (OR CAN
GUESS), USING THE 3D TOPOLOGICAL RELIEF MAPS
YOU SAW ON PLATEAU ISLAND, WHERE ON EACH
ISLAND EACH FIRE MARBLE DOME IS. SOME
GUESSWORK IS UNAVOIDABLE, UNFORTUNATELY.
ONE COLOR IS MISSING, AND YOU HAVE NOT
YET VISITED ONE ISLAND. SO YOU DON'T KNOW
PRECISELY WHERE THE FIFTH FIRE MARBLE
DOME IS LOCATED.*

SOLVING THE FIRE MARBLE PUZZLE

Once you find the Fire Marble Puzzle, in the upper level of the
Golden Dome, accessed by way of the elevated bridge from
Position 3 in the Gate Room, you can try to solve it. The puzzle
consists of arrays of twenty-five holes in each of twenty-five
larger squares.

► You've seen this pattern of squares before.

► Once, this world was a single large island. Because
  Gehn's worlds do not last, at some point in the past the
  original continent was "riven" into five unequal pieces.

► Can you picture the graphic outlines of each island on
  the large array?

► Can you further plot the locations of the Fire Marble
  Domes on the different island shapes?

► You should have worked out the geography of each
  dome back on Plateau Island.

► You may need to return to Plateau Island and study
  the maps in the Map Room again, paying particular
  attention to where each Fire Marble Dome is located.

► The puzzle provides you with six colored marbles.

► You only need five. There's one extra. Which might it
  be?

▶ Try placing each of the five colored marbles in the appropriate holes. When you think you have it right, go back down the passageway to the switch on the wall. Press the switch, and something that resembles an enormous press will come down and cover the marble array. When a white button appears under the switch, click on it.

IF YOU HAVE THE RIGHT COLORED MARBLES IN THE CORRECT PLACES, SOMETHING LIKE A HUGE EXPLOSION—A RUSH OF AIR AND POWER—WILL FILL THE PASSAGEWAY, TUGGING AT DANGLING CABLES AND OTHER LOOSE PARTS. IF YOU HAVE IT WRONG, NOTHING WILL HAPPEN. TRY GOING BACK TO THE MARBLE ARRAY AND SETTING UP ANOTHER PATTERN.

When you have the right combination and hear and see that rush of wind, you have successfully provided power to all of the linking books. You can go to any Fire Marble Dome now, access its linking book, and travel to Gehn's hide-away age.

GEHN'S WORLD

When you open one of the linking books inside a Fire Marble Dome, you will get a glimpse of another world...a strange, red-lit world of pyramidal growths, with a structure of some kind atop one of the largest. This is a different Age or world created by Gehn as the location of his private dwelling.

Touch the image, and you are transported to Gehn's home...and for the second time in your quest, you find yourself behind bars.

Other linking books are visible around the cage, each identified by its own island graphic. None of them is powered, however. A plate with a star symbol is on the bars of your cage. When you press the button in the center of the plate, Gehn will appear for a little chat.

▶ He seems friendly enough. And eager to impress you with the fact that you have probably heard incorrect information about him.

▶ If you have not reacquired the Trap Book from the Moiety, he will ask you to find it for him—not realizing its true nature.

▶ If you have reacquired the Trap Book—which he thinks is a linking book back to D'ni—he will consider using it...but ask you to go through first.

▶ If you trap Gehn before he powers up the Linking Books, you'll have to find the power switch yourself.

▶ If you do not touch the book, he will give you time to think about it. He will also turn on the power to the Linking Books around your cage, allowing you free access to any part of Riven. He does ask you, however, to refrain from visiting Catherine, whom he's been forced to separate from the rebels, for her safety as well as his.

▶ Can you deduce which symbol represents Catherine's Prison Island?

▶ Whom do you trust now? Atrus, who sent you on this quest in the first place? Catherine, the leader of the Rebel Moiety, a woman you've never met? Or Gehn, who admits to having tried to kill his son once, but who now is trying to make amends...and who needs your help to save Riven and its people?

BY NOW, THROUGH YOUR EXPLORATIONS AND BY READING THE JOURNALS OF ATRUS, CATHERINE, AND GEHN, YOU SHOULD HAVE FORMED AN IDEA ABOUT WHO IS TELLING THE TRUTH, WHO TO BELIEVE, AND WHO TO HELP.

PRISON ISLAND

The fifth island of Riven is a tiny speck lost in a vast expanse of sea, so far from the other four islands that you cannot even see it on the horizon. Most of the island is embraced by the stump of a titanic tree, with roots cradling naked rock and extending into the sea. A building—Catherine's prison—rises from the stump.

YOU WILL HAVE TO FACE GEHN AGAIN AND GET HIM TO USE THE TRAP BOOK IN ORDER TO RESCUE CATHERINE AND WIN THE GAME.

IT IS ALSO POSSIBLE TO TRAP GEHN BEFORE VISITING CATHERINE. IF YOU CAN FIND THE CODE TO HER CELL BEFORE VISITING PRISON ISLAND, YOU CAN RESCUE HER IMMEDIATELY.

END GAME

Use the Fire Marble Dome outside Catherine's prison to return to Gehn's home. You can summon him again by clicking on the button that has reset itself on the bars to your cage. You now have two goals: get Gehn to use the Trap Book, and learn the combination to the lock on Catherine's prison.

THE TRAP BOOK

Gehn must touch the image on the Trap Book
for it to imprison him.

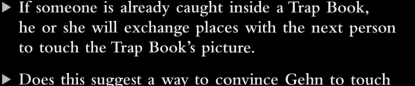

- ▶ How does a Trap Book work?

- ▶ If you've played the game Myst, you've
  used Trap Books before. Atrus's sons,
  Sirrus and Achenar, you may recall, had
  been caught inside Trap Books and were trying to
  escape.

- ▶ If someone is already caught inside a Trap Book,
  he or she will exchange places with the next person
  to touch the Trap Book's picture.

- ▶ Does this suggest a way to convince Gehn to touch
  the image?

THE CODE TO THE PRISON

Once you've exchanged places with Gehn, you are outside the
bars and have access to his quarters. A lever on one window
ledge lowers the bars of your cage, giving you access to all five
books.

- ▶ You will have to search for the code.

- ▶ It is likely to be well-hidden.

- ▶ The code wasn't in his journal in the lab. If the secret
  is anywhere, it must be here.

- ▶ Search his home carefully. (He won't be coming back
  to interrupt you, certainly!)

- ▶ The ladder rungs lead to his bedroom downstairs.

- ▶ His bedroom contains lots of odds and ends pertain-
  ing to his private life.

- ▶ You are searching for something that gives you a clue
  to the series of sounds that will open the lock to
  Catherine's prison.

Once you have the code, you can return to Catherine's prison
and free her. She tells you that Riven is doomed, that what you
must do now is signal Atrus by using the telescope to crack
open the Star Fissure, sealed over now by metal plates. While

you do that, she will arrange to get the Rivenese natives to safety in the Rebel Age.

CHECK GEHN'S PERSONAL BELONGINGS CAREFULLY. HE WOULDN'T LEAVE INFORMATION LIKE THIS IN A JOURNAL. THE CLUE WILL BE HIDDEN WHERE HE CAN EASILY GET AT IT.

IF YOU TRAP GEHN BEFORE HE TURNS ON THE POWER TO THE LINKING BOOKS, YOU'LL HAVE TO FIND THE LEVER THAT TURNS ON THE POWER YOURSELF.

By the time you reach the Prison Island's Fire Marble Dome, it is closed and turning again, evidence that Catherine has used it to escape first to Gehn's world, then to one of the islands of Riven. You must go through and, somehow, use the telescope to open the Star Fissure.

THE TELESCOPE

Yes! The strange device you first encountered on Riven was a telescope, of sorts, and now its operation is the key to your escape.

- ▶ Do the controls work? Have you turned on the power?

- ▶ If you haven't, you'd better do so. Where might the power be coming from?

- ▶ Is the pipe leading to the device on the right side of the apparatus a clue? Where does the pipe come from?

- ▶ Have you opened the hatch cover on the ground?

- ▶ Have you learned where the combination might be recorded?

- ▶ Who might have that combination?

- ▶ When you rescue Catherine from the Prison Island, she tells you where the combination is, and what you must do.

- ▶ Okay, you've got power, the controls work. You're trying to lower the telescope to break the glass and open the Star Fissure. Something seems to be blocking the telescope as it slides down the mounting rails.

- ▶ Check the supports carefully.

- ▶ There's a clue in Catherine's journal.

- ▶ What you're trying to do is not normally a good idea— break the glass and open the fissure. Isn't it likely that some sort of safety feature might have been built into the thing?

- ▶ Look for a pin blocking the telescope's movement and move it out of the way.

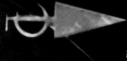

WARNING! DON'T TRY TO OPERATE THIS DEVICE UNTIL YOU'RE SUPPOSED TO, AT THE VERY END OF THE GAME, OR YOU'RE IN REAL TROUBLE!

Remember lab class at the microscope in school, turning the focus and accidentally driving the objective lens down through the glass slide? This is what you are attempting to do. You must open the window—take a moment to look at the stars mysteriously evident through the port, focusing on them through the eyepiece—and then use the lever and the button to the right to drive the tip of the device down through the glass.

You've done it! The glass cracks, and first the steel plating, then the entire telescope and its supporting structure topple into the whirlwind fury of the open fissure. Riven is dying, crumbling around you as the sky grows black and the ground trembles. Atrus, summoned from D'ni, appears...and, a moment later, Catherine joins him. The natives are safe, and the universes need not fear Gehn's further misguided meddling...

...if, of course, you succeeded in both trapping Gehn and freeing Catherine. The ending will be quite different if you've failed somewhere along the line.

That, of course, is why you bought this guide! Go back and try Riven again. Enjoy the complex beauty of this alien world.

And this time see if you can open the gateway to a better world...

Chapter Four

THE ISLANDS OF RIVEN: MAPS AND SPECIFICS

This is a Sunner chapter. It contains both hints and tips for playing the game, and specific hints for solving certain key puzzles. Reading this chapter before playing Riven will rob the game of some of its fun and suspense.

As is the case with Chapter 3, this chapter is divided into sections describing each area within Riven. This time, however, each area is mapped out in detail. You can use these maps to determine where you are, where you've been, and where you want to go... but you'll definitely lose some of the mystery and suspense along the way.

Also included in this chapter are lists of the puzzles and problems that must be solved if you are to proceed through the game, along with some specific hints and tips for solving them. It stops short of giving away the entire solution to each problem, but it definitely gives away an awful lot!

TEMPLE ISLAND

You start the adventure on Temple Island, south of the Star Fissure and the Telescope. You must untangle the mysteries of the Gate Room, the Great Golden Dome, and the Temple.

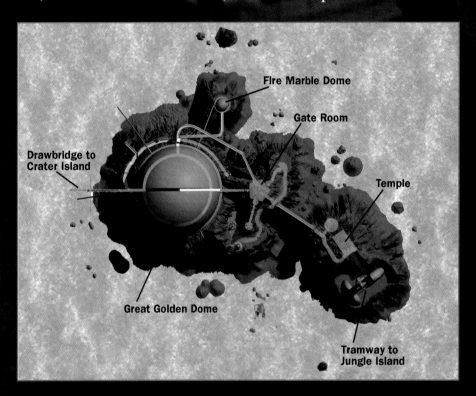

PUZZLES AND PROBLEMS ON TEMPLE ISLAND

▶ Solve the puzzle of the Gate Room. How do you get where you need to go, and open the gates and grates you need to open?

▶ Provide power to the telescope.

▶ How do you reach the Golden Dome?

▶ What can you turn on in the Golden Dome?

▶ What can you turn on beyond the Golden Dome?

▶ The Temple. What can you learn about its designer? How do you open the outer Temple door?

After Completing Your Explorations of Temple Island, You Should Have:

- ▶ Figured out how to use the Gate Room to access any of the five doors.

- ▶ Lowered the grates that block two of the doors.

- ▶ Turned on the power to the telescope.

- ▶ Explored the Golden Dome and switched on power to the West Drawbridge to Crater Island and the drawbridge between the Gate Room and the Golden Dome.

- ▶ Opened the main door of the Temple and found the Tram to Jungle Island.

You may also have seen the spinning Temple Island Fire Marble Dome from a distance, but you won't be able to reach it until a later visit.

PUZZLES AND PROBLEMS ON JUNGLE ISLAND

Ride the mag-lev tram from Temple Island to Jungle Island. This area is larger and has a lot more in the way of secrets and mysteries than did Temple Island.

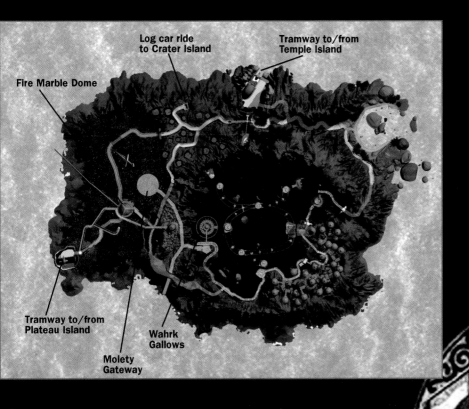

Log car ride to Crater Island

Tramway to/from Temple Island

Fire Marble Dome

Tramway to/from Plateau Island

Wahrk Gallows

Molety Gateway

- ▶ What is the purpose of the wooden eyes?

- ▶ Can you link each eye with a particular animal, through a particular sound the animal makes and/or through the silhouette of that animal?

- ▶ Can you find four wooden eyes?

- ▶ Can you find a place where you can learn the meaning of the symbols on the back of each wooden eye?

- ▶ Figure out how to lower the submarine, and then how to operate it to travel around Village Lake.

- ▶ The Control Room: Can you find a way to lower three of five ladders to gain access to key landings around the inside of Village Lake?

- ▶ The School Room: Can you learn what you need to know about D'ni numbers?

- ▶ The Wahrk Gallows: You must close the central opening on the Wahrk Gallows before you can explore all of its secrets.

- ▶ What is the secret of the Wahrk Idol in the jungle? Can you find a way through to reach the catwalks you can see among the trees, or the Fire Marble Dome you see turning above you?

- ▶ There is actually more than one way of getting to the Fire Marble Dome. When you do reach it, can you stop it from turning, and learn the symbol associated with it?

- ▶ After penetrating the Wahrk Idol's secret, can you find Gehn's raised throne? What can you do there that you must do to continue your explorations?

- ▶ Found the Wahrk Idol. You may have learned its secret the first time around, or you may need to come back to Jungle Island later, from an unexpected direction.

- ▶ Now, or later, you will need to reach the Jungle Island Fire Marble Dome, learn the appropriate symbol, and visit Gehn's throne, which you must do to gain access to the Wahrk Gallows.

- ▶ After accessing the Wahrk Gallows, you can find Gehn's prison, solve the problem of finding the gateway to the Moiety Age, and at least begin thinking about how to solve that devious puzzle.

PUZZLES AND PROBLEMS ON CRATER ISLAND

You ride the log car to another island, this one known as Crater Island. You arrive rather unceremoniously, dumped down a chute and dropped into a chipper that, fortunately for you, is unpowered at the moment.

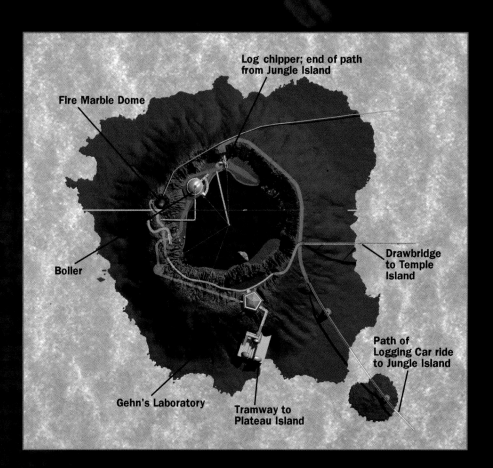

Log chipper; end of path from Jungle Island

Fire Marble Dome

Boiler

Drawbridge to Temple Island

Path of Logging Car ride to Jungle Island

Gehn's Laboratory

Tramway to Plateau Island

▶ Can you solve the puzzle of the boiler? To reach the ladder and passageway in the center of the room beyond the door, you must raise the floor grating, ensuring that the tank is drained of water and that the furnace is off. How do you go about doing this?

▶ After raising the grating and crossing to the drainage pipe in the middle of the boiler tank, you can take a long, black crawl and climb that will deposit you high atop the mountains ringing the lake. Can you find a path leading over the crest of the ridge and down to a railed balcony?

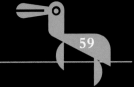
▶ The apparatus at the end of the long catwalk leading into the mountain is for catching frogs. Can you catch one, using the trap and the bait?

▶ The large building visible on the cliff side is Gehn's book-making laboratory. The only door you can reach is locked. Getting in is a problem, requiring an approach from an unexpected direction.

▶ The double doors above the railed balcony on the cliff lead to the frog-catching apparatus, but there's more to this site than meets the eye. Can you find the Fire Marble Dome for Crater Island, and can you find the hidden kinetoscope that stops it?

TIP

THERE'S QUITE A LOT THAT'S INTERESTING IN GEHN'S LAB, WHERE HE HAS OBVIOUSLY BEEN EXPERIMENTING WITH HOW TO MAKE PAPER AND BIND BOOKS. YOU MIGHT ALSO GUESS WHY HE'S BEEN CATCHING FROGS: HE TAKES AN EXTRACT FROM THEM AND SMOKES IT IN HIS PIPE. YES, OUR FRIEND GEHN SMOKES FROG EXTRACT, SLAUGHTERING HUN-DREDS OF THE TINY, BEAUTIFUL CREATURES TO FEED HIS HABIT. HIS JOURNAL DISCUSSES HIS SEARCH FOR A BETTER, SMOOTHER FROG EXTRACT. WHAT DOES THIS TELL YOU ABOUT THE MAN?

After penetrating Gehn's laboratory, you must access an important source of additional clues that you'll need in your quest. Also, there's an open path leading back to the Golden Dome via the bridge, or you can return to Jungle Island on the log cart, or you can summon a tram from the front of Gehn's lab.

AFTER COMPLETING YOUR EXPLORATIONS OF CRATER ISLAND, YOU SHOULD HAVE:

▶ Solved the puzzles of the boiler, the central power valve, and the ventilation fan duct.

▶ Discovered the location of this island's Fire Marble Dome.

▶ Found and read Gehn's lab journal.

▶ Found in Gehn's lab journal a series of Rivenese numbers.

▶ Found the catwalk and bridge leading back to the Great
Golden Dome on Temple Island.

▶ Found the tram outside Gehn's lab.

▶ Learned quite a lot about Gehn and his personal habits.

The tram takes you to the next unexplored island, Plateau Island.

PUZZLES AND PROBLEMS ON PLATEAU ISLAND

The tram from Gehn's lab deposits you on Plateau Island. Note that, although you can get out on the left side of the tram, there is a door visible to the right. Take the left-hand side for now, but be thinking about how you can get across to the other side of the tram line.

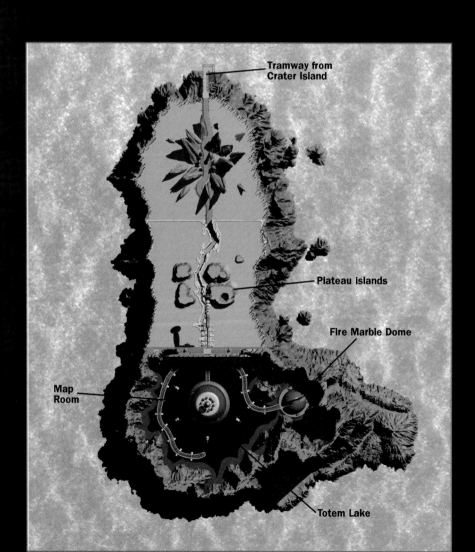

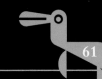

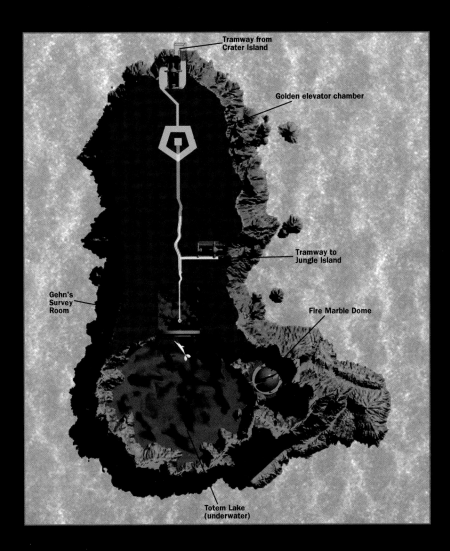

Tramway from
Crater Island

Golden elevator chamber

Tramway to
Jungle Island

Gehn's
Survey
Room

Fire Marble Dome

Totem Lake
(underwater)

Plateau Island contains some of the grandest and most spectacular
scenery yet seen in the world of Riven. It also holds the key to
the most fiendish of Riven's puzzles.

▶ The overhead view of the plateau
islands and the corresponding 3-D relief
views of each sector of each island in
the Map Room together constitute
both problem and puzzle. What are you
supposed to do with the information
displayed here?

▶ This island's Fire Marble Dome is visi-
ble turning beyond a cleft in the rock wall beyond the
lake on which the Map Room rests. The kinetoscope,
when you find it, is broken. Can you open the dome
anyway?

▶ Can you figure out how to reach the other side of the tram?

▶ The Viewing Chamber Puzzles. When you reach the other side, you will encounter one of Gehn's scribes, and, if you pursue him, you will watch him vanish in another tram car— but not the one you arrived in. The passageway beyond the tram car station, however, leads to an underwater viewing chamber which offers several important clues to several of Riven's other puzzles. Can you find them?

AFTER FINISHING WITH PLATEAU ISLAND, YOU SHOULD:

▶ Have a good guess as to the identity of the fifth animal shape, which will enable you to solve the Moiety Puzzle on Jungle Island.

▶ Have noted the Fire Marble symbols and matched most of them with a different color. This will help you solve the Gehn's Age Puzzle.

▶ Have learned which patterns of squares represent which islands.

▶ Have solved the Map Puzzle and identified which sector on each island holds a Fire Marble Dome. This, too, is necessary for the solution to the puzzle of Gehn's Age.

▶ Taken the newly discovered tram back to Jungle Island, and learned the Wahrk Idol's secret, if you didn't find it earlier.

PUZZLES AND PROBLEMS OF REACHING THE MOIETY AGE

You reach the Moiety Age from Jungle Island. Once you get there, a woman named Nelah gives you Catherine's journal and the Trap Book that was taken from you at the beginning of your quest.

Collecting all of the clues you need, however, is a bit of a chore.

▶ Can you solve the problem of finding the gateway to the Moiety Age? You need to learn how to use the submarine to reach the Wahrk Gallows. You also need to have found Gehn's Throne and learned how to close the base of the gallows. Then you must find your way up the gallows to the prison cell, learn the cell's secret, find your way through the darkness, find out how to light your way back, and finally (!) discover the doorway to the gateway.

▶ After finding the gateway, you must know the code for opening it. You must have found and examined four wooden eyes at various points in Jungle Island, and associated each with a particular animal silhouette or, in one case, with the call of an animal that you have seen on the island. You must have associated

each animal with a symbol that you've discovered, after visiting the School Room, is a number.

▶ With four animals and four numbers, you're almost there, but you also need to discover what the fifth animal silhouette is, in the underwater viewing chamber on Plateau Island. You will not be able to reach the wooden eye associated with this silhouette, but you will be able to learn which number is associated with it in Gehn's lab.

▶ Finally, you must touch the proper stones in the gateway room in the proper order. The order is obvious, based on the number associated with each silhouette. If you get the order or the animal graphic wrong, nothing happens, and you must reset the stones by touching each in any order. When you have the right stones in the correct order, the water covering the far wall flows away through side channels, the dagger panel opens, and you will be able to reach a linking book that takes you to the Moiety Age.

You will be knocked unconscious by a rebel blowgun dart and awaken in a small chamber. At this point, all you need to do is guess what the woman is telling you to do, and do it.

AFTER FINISHING THE REBEL AGE, YOU SHOULD HAVE:

▶ The Trap Book taken from you at the beginning of the quest.

▶ Catherine's journal, which contains information you will need later.

The woman will return with another linking book. Touch the image on the book, and you will be returned to the room of the Twenty-five Stones on Jungle Island.

PUZZLES AND PROBLEMS OF REACHING GEHN'S AGE

Reaching the alternate reality where Gehn lives when he is not playing god and lording it over the inhabitants of Riven, involves some of the toughest puzzles in the game.

▶ Can you learn the first part of the secret of the Fire Marble Domes, and open the outer shell?

▶ Can you acquire the five-digit code that opens the inner lock and gives you access to a linking book?

▶ Have you learned how to read the D'ni symbols for the numerals 1 through 10? Having done that, can you figure out the pattern the numbers use in order to figure out the numerals 11 through 24? Finally, there is a chance that one symbol represents the numeral 25. If that numeral occurs in the sequence, can you guess what it is?

▶ Have you associated a particular graphic symbol with each of four domes?

▶ Have you learned what colors are represented by those symbols?

▶ Have you reached the Map Room on Plateau Island, learned its secrets, and plotted the locations of five Fire Marble Domes in Riven? Four of these are relatively easy, a fifth is tougher.

▶ Have you solved the Marble Puzzle, which turns on the power to the linking books? You must correctly place five out of six colored marbles on a grid of 625 holes. You will only know three of the colors for certain; the fourth and fifth require a guesswork choice among the three remaining marbles. You will also be uncertain of the position of the fifth marble, although the island involved is quite small, limiting your possible choices.

If the correct marbles are in the proper holes, when you pull the lever on the wall and then press a white button, an explosion of air around the marble device indicates that the linking books are now powered and ready to use.

Once you reach Gehn's Age, what happens next depends on whether or not you have reached the Moiety Age and reacquired the Trap Book. You will have the opportunity to come and go among the five different islands of Riven and, if you have not yet done so, you must solve the problem of reaching the Rebel Age to reacquire your stolen Trap Book. You may also visit  Catherine on Prison Island, but each time you will return to Gehn's Age, until either you successfully trap him or he kills you.

After Finishing Gehn's Age, You Should Have:

► Solved the Marble Puzzle that gives you access to Gehn's Age through any of the Fire Marble Domes.

► Found yourself in a prison cell in Gehn's home.

► Seen the five linking books arrayed about your prison cell, and recognized each as a link—initially unpowered—to one of the five islands of Riven.

► Found a button that calls Gehn into the room for a little chat.

► Listened to Gehn and either watched him turn on the power for all of the linking books or trapped him, escaped from the cage, and turned on the power for yourself.

► Used the Trap Book to capture Gehn, and escape from your cell. This might be accomplished on a subsequent trip, rather than during the first visit to this Age.

► Used the linking book to the fifth island to go and visit Catherine, and seen the coded lock on her cell. This might be accomplished on this visit, or on a later one.

► Found the key—a series of specific sounds—somewhere in Gehn's residence that enables you to open Catherine's cell.

► Returned to Catherine's island and freed her.

Don't give up now! You're almost there!

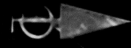

WARNING! WHEN YOU SUMMON GEHN, HE TAKES THE TRAP BOOK FROM YOU AND THEN OFFERS YOU THE OPPORTUNITY OF GOING THROUGH AHEAD OF HIM. YOU MAY REFUSE. HE WILL ONLY GIVE YOU THREE CHANCES, HOWEVER, BEFORE HE DECIDES THAT YOU ARE NOT WORTH THE EFFORT, AND HE KILLS YOU.

PUZZLES AND PROBLEMS OF CATHERINE'S ISLAND

Although Gehn asks you not to, there is nothing stopping you from using the linking book outside your cell in his residence to journey to Prison Island where Catherine is being held prisoner. You can talk to Catherine, but you will not be able to free her from her prison cell unless you can crack the code to the three-keyed lock you encounter in the elevator.

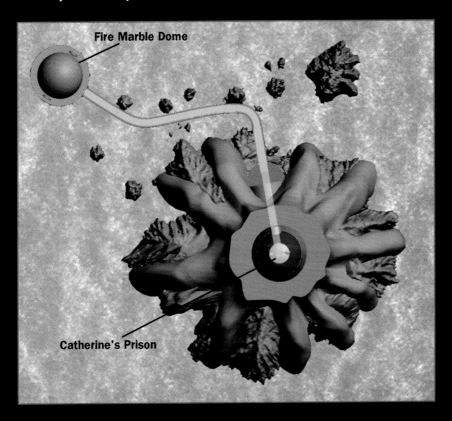

Fire Marble Dome

Catherine's Prison

▶ Can you find the code to the lock somewhere in Gehn's residence? You can only do this if you've successfully trapped him in Atrus's Trap Book.

▶ Can you find the lever that opens your former cell? You need to open the cage in order to regain access to the five linking books.

AFTER LEAVING CATHERINE'S ISLAND FOR THE LAST TIME, YOU SHOULD HAVE:

▶ Freed Catherine from her cell.

▶ Received instructions from her regarding the telescope and the Star Fissure. You will need to solve one final puzzle before you successfully complete the game.

THE TELESCOPE PUZZLE

You have one last puzzle to face, now... and ironically it's within a handful of steps from the very spot at which you first arrived on Riven. The telescope is the device that looks something like a steel ice cream cone suspended above a round hatch set into some iron plates on the ground. An eyepiece gives you a view of the hatch... or of what's beyond it, presumably, if the hatch is open. A button raises or lowers the telescope for focus; a lever determines which way—up or down—the device moves.

Your goal is to open the hatch, revealing a glass window looking into a field of stars within a deep fissure in the ground, and then use the tip of the telescope to break the glass and end the Riven Age.

▶ Have you figured out how to turn on the power to the telescope?

▶ Have you learned where the code to the hatch's locking device is kept, and used it to open the hatch?

▶ Have you found the locking pin that protects the glass from the telescope's descent?

▶ Have you smashed the glass?

YOU HAVE COMPLETED YOUR FINAL TASK WHEN YOU HAVE:

▶ Powered up the telescope.

▶ Unlocked the safety pin.

▶ Used the telescope to break the glass.

A few moments after Riven's final Armageddon has commenced, Atrus appears. What happens next, and what he says, depend upon whether or not you have successfully done everything required of you, or whether some tasks remain unfinished when you finally open the Star Fissure.

You Will Have Won the Most Complete Victory Possible If When You Open the Star Fissure, You Have:

▶ Trapped Gehn.

▶ Freed Catherine.

If either or both of these tasks remain unfinished, you will be treated to a different ending, one less joyful than that resulting from complete success.

Chapter Five

PUZZLES AND PROBLEMS:
THE SOLUTIONS

This is a Wahrk chapter. It lists each of the major problems and puzzles within Riven and presents all of the solutions, with no attempt at concealing them. DON'T READ THIS CHAPTER, don't even page through it, if you want to have a chance of solving Riven's puzzles on your own!

THE GATE ROOM

▶ The Gate Room is a five-sided chamber that rotates 72 degrees clockwise each time you press one of the rotation buttons at the outer doorways.

▶ The Gate Room has two open doorways. It rotates within a chamber that possesses five possible gateways. As the inner room turns, it opens connections between a different pair of gateways with each rotation.

▶ The five possible gateways are labeled 1 through 5. Position 1 is the first gate, on the southeast wall, which you encounter at the beginning of the game. The first time you enter the room, the open doors connect positions 1 and 3.

▶ Each time you press the rotation button, the inner chamber turns by one of its five sides.

▶ From position 1, you can access position 3. If you rotate the room three times, you can access position 4.

▶ When you first encounter the Gate Room, lowered grates at positions 3 and 4 block your access to the only two doors you can reach from position 1. The switch to raise the grate at position 4 is at position 2, and the one to raise the position 3 grate is at position 4. You need to access one of the other positions and go through in order to rotate the room again and gain access to the other gates.

▶ To do this, first press the rotation button at position 1 four times to open the doorways at 5 and at 2. (You are heading for position 5, which is the one position that does not have a rotation button.) Then follow the outside path around and down to the wooden gate on the east side of the building. Click on the ground beneath the locked gate to crawl underneath and get into the cave beyond. Go up through the cave to the open doorway. Go through to position 2, where you will find the switch for raising the grate at position 4, as well as the power valve for turning on the power to the telescope outside.

▶ The geometry of the gate room resembles the following:

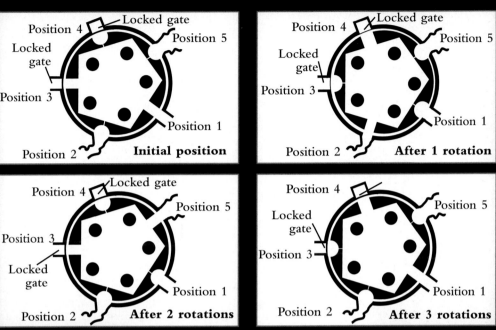

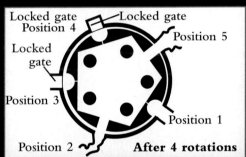

▶ From position 2, rotate the inner room twice, to align open doors at positions 2 and 4. Go through to 4 where you will find the switch to raise the grate blocking position 3. A door locked from the other side prevents you from accessing position 4. Instead, from position 4, rotate the room two more times to connect positions 4 and 1. Go through to 1 and rotate twice. This opens the doors at 1 and 3, just as they were when you first entered this room. However, now the grate that was frustrating you at 3 is raised and you can continue your explorations in that direction.

THE MAGNETIC TRAM

▶ The trams you encounter on Riven are fairly straightforward and easy to figure out. A few points need to be kept in mind.

▶ The knob to the side of the main, central control rotates the car 180 degrees. Move it to the right or left to put the tram in position to go.

▶ The lever in the center makes the tram go. Once this switch is thrown, travel is automatic.

▶ Near each tram station is a silver sphere atop a stand or pedestal, with a blue button or press-plate at the top. You can press this to call a tram, if no tram is waiting for you at the station.

▶ On Plateau Island, use the tram's rotation ability to enable you to turn in place—and thereby reach a door that is otherwise inaccessible.

THE SUBMARINE

▶ To lower the submarine into the water, follow the paths and piers counterclockwise around Village Lake on Jungle Island until you reach the Village. Continue climbing ladders and follow the path until you reach the highest point beyond the Village, a ceremonial area where the submarine has been raised on a kind of elevator platform. Throw the lever to lower the sub into the water.

▶ Proceed back the way you came, down the ladders to the pier, and then clockwise around the lake, past the Jungle, past the clear-cut, past the rope bridge, all the way down the stone steps past Sunner Rock, and then through a tunnel to emerge once again above the island's central lake. Go down the ladder beyond the Beetle Pool and follow ladders and paths as far as you can go, until you reach the ladder going down into the submarine.

▶ Note that the submarine's stopping points are located in literal holes in the water. Some quirk of the physical laws of this universe enable the water in this world to be shaped at will, creating holes and other peculiar, watery constructs. By studying the surface of the central lake from some elevated vantage point, you can deduce where the submarine stopping places are located.

▶ The submarine controls are simple. The rotating lever turns the sub around. The lever at the bottom can be moved left or right, and determines which fork in the tracks you will take when you move forward across a switch or track crossing. The lever to the right moves the sub forward to the next decision point.

▶ The submarine moves on wheels along an underwater track. The track configuration is as follows:

▶ Before you can enter or leave the submarine, a ladder must be extended from an access pier above the water. The first time you enter the sub, only the ladders at the sub dock and the control tower are extended. You must go from the sub dock to the tower dock, leave the sub, and then climb a high ladder up the cliff to the control room to raise the levers that extend the other three ladders.

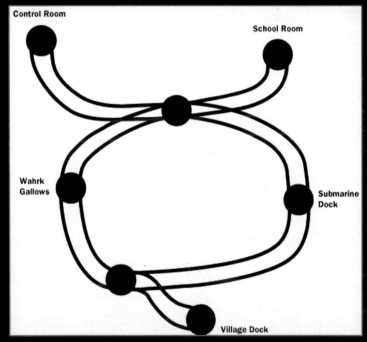

Control Room

School Room

Wahrk
Gallows

Submarine
Dock

Village Dock

▶ With all ladders accessible, you can now get to any of the five sites around the lake. From the sub dock or the village pier, you can leave the submarine and continue your travels elsewhere; the control tower and the school room, while important, are dead ends. Once you leave, you can only return to the sub.

▶ The Wahrk Gallows is a special case. The first time you leave the sub here, you can walk around the open base of the gallows, but you can't go anywhere else. Pulling the triangular handle on the chain lowers a bar on a rope, but you cannot reach it and after a moment or two, the rope automatically rises again. After you find your way to Gehn's Throne high above the Wahrk Gallows, you can close the base of the gallows, and then return to the gallows via

submarine, lower the bar and ride it to the top, and find a
ladder that you can lower to the lakeside walkway. When
this task is complete, you can leave your sub at the gallows
and continue your explorations elsewhere as well.

THE WAHRK IDOL

▶ At the end of a path in the jungle is a huge, brightly
painted wooden construction that appears to be some
kind of idol or religious totem designed to look like a
wahrk. The path seems to end there.

▶ Face the idol, while standing between two posts or dec-
orations with rounded tops. Touch the top of the right-
hand post. This raises a switch which opens the wahrk
idol's mouth.

▶ Follow the stairs up into the idol. A lever closes the
mouth or opens it again. Beyond that
point, an elevator can take you up to the
jungle catwalks, Gehn's Throne, and the
island's Fire Marble Dome, or down to the
mag-tram that
can transport you to Plateau Island.

▶ You can first penetrate the idol when you
arrive here from Plateau Island. When you
emerge from the idol's mouth, you will
see the raised switch on the post to your left. Clicking
on the switch closes the idol's mouth once more.

THE WAHRK GALLOWS

▶ To get to the Moiety Age, you must get past the Wahrk
Gallows.

▶ Use the submarine to reach the control tower dock.
Climb up to the control tower, and raise all the levers to
extend all of the ladders.

▶ When you learn the secret of the Wahrk Idol, follow
the catwalk past the Jungle Island Fire Marble Dome
and find the tower housing Gehn's Throne Room.
Throw the left-hand lever to raise the throne, and then
throw the right-hand lever to close the base of the
Wahrk Gallows, which enables access across the base.

▶ Use the submarine to reach the gallows and exit there. Cross to the center of the (now closed) base and pull the triangular handle on a chain.

▶ A bar hanging from a rope lowers. Grab the bar and ride it up to the top.

▶ From here, you can lower a ladder to the pier to ensure future access. You can also find the prison cell and its prisoner, and from here find your way through a secret passage to the Moiety Gateway Room.

D'NI NUMBERS

▶ Learn how to count in fluent D'ni by using the sub to reach the school room. Play the wahrk counting game to learn the first 10 digits. Use the patterns you find here to deduce the numbers 11 through 25.

▶ The D'ni use a base five counting system. In the base 10 system, which we use, we have distinct numerals for 1 through 9, with 10 represented as a 1 with a zero to the right of it to show a 1 in the tens' place. Count up another 10 and 20 is written as a 2 with a zero to the right to put it in the tens' place. In the D'ni system, they have unique symbols for 1 through 4, then build on these through rotation and combination to create higher numerals.

▶ The D'ni numerals from 1 to 5 are:

Note that 5 is, in effect, a 1 rotated 90 degrees counterclockwise. (Yes, it could also have been rotated clockwise, but bear with us!)

| 1 | 2 | 3 | 4 | 5 |

▶ The numerals 6 through 9 are created by combining 5 plus one of the first 4 numerals. Thus, 9 is 5 + 4.

▶ The numeral 10 is a 2 rotated 90 degrees counterclockwise.

▶ The numerals 11 through 14 are made by combining 10 plus one of the first four numerals. Thus 12 is 10 + 2.

▶ The number 15 is made by rotating a 3 counterclockwise 90 degrees.

▶ The numerals 16 through 19 are made by combining 15 plus one of the first four numerals. Thus 18 is 15 + 3. Note that two of the lines in the figure are contiguous and look like a single line.

▶ The number 20 is a 4 rotated 90 degrees counterclockwise.

▶ The numerals 21 through 24 are made by combining 20 with one of the first four numerals: 21 is 20 + 1.

▶ The symbol for 25 is different.

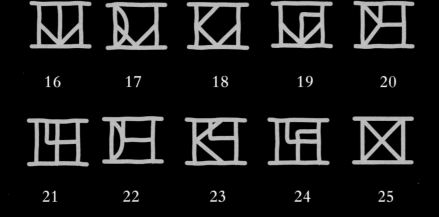

16   17   18   19   20

21   22   23   24   25

have the numerals written side by side. For example,
the code string 3 - 7 - 8 - 11 - 22 would be written:

▶ While exploring Riven, you should be on the lookout

3   7   8   11   22

for D'ni numerals. They always mean something
important!

THE BOILER

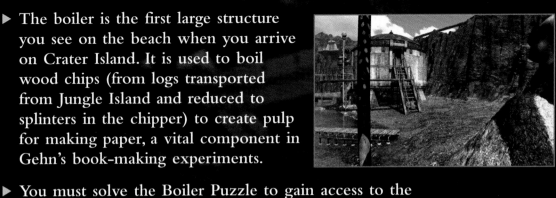

- ▶ The boiler is the first large structure you see on the beach when you arrive on Crater Island. It is used to boil wood chips (from logs transported from Jungle Island and reduced to splinters in the chipper) to create pulp for making paper, a vital component in Gehn's book-making experiments.

- ▶ You must solve the Boiler Puzzle to gain access to the boiler tank, cross a raised floor grating to a ladder leading down a drain in the center, and eventually reach the mountaintop, where you can attempt to enter Gehn's laboratory.

- ▶ The boiler is powered from a pipe extending into the center of the lake. To power the boiler and operate the controls, you must follow the walkway out to the middle of the lake and set the steam valve lever to the middle of the three possible positions.

- ▶ You will need to set the boiler controls a certain way to gain access to the tank's interior and the ladder in the center.

- ▶ The first control you encounter is on the left of the walkway around the boiler building as you approach the main controls. There's a valve lever that can be set to one of two positions. The higher/farther position powers the water pumps for filling and emptying the boiler. The lower/nearer position powers the grating.

- ▶ The main controls—the one in front of you as you face the tank—consist of a wheel to the left which fills or drains the tank, a lever to the right which turns the furnace on or off, and a switch to the upper right that raises or lowers a grate inside the tank.

- ▶ To enter the boiler, the furnace must be turned off. When it is on, you will hear a roar, a red light will be visible by the boiler door, and the door itself will be locked.

- ▶ To enter, the tank must be empty. Make sure the power at the Y junction is switched to the far/high pipe. Turn the large wheel to move the pipe, and watch through the vertical glass view port to see the water drain away.

▶ To enter the boiler and get across to the ladder, the floor grating must be raised. Make sure the valve at the Y-junction is set to the nearer/lower branch. Throw the switch at the upper right, and watch the grate rise into position. If the grate was up and you've just lowered it, throw the switch again to reposition the grate.

▶ With the furnace turned off, the tank empty, and the grate raised, you can enter the boiler tank and reach the ladder.

GEHN'S LABORATORY

▶ To reach Gehn's laboratory on Crater Island, you must go through the following steps.

▶ Go through the drain pipe after solving the Boiler Puzzle described above. Emerge on the mountain and follow a path across the rocks and down onto a railed platform on the cliff face.

▶ Open the round hatch, which was locked from underneath. This gives you access to the beach and the boiler again, if you should need it.

▶ Go through the double doors. Close the doors to reveal hidden passageways to the left and right.

▶ As you face the doors from inside, follow the right-hand passage. Find a lever against the rocks and pull it, which turns off the ventilation fans inside. (This walkway also leads you to the front of Gehn's lab, which is locked, and then to the West Drawbridge and the Great Golden Dome.)

▶ Return to the double doors and turn left. Follow the steps down to the frog-catching chamber.

▶ With the ventilator fans turned off, you can click on the grating above the frog trap apparatus to open the shaft and crawl inside.

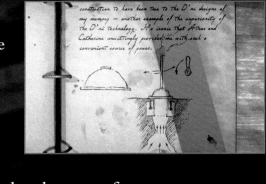

- ▶ Follow the ventilator shaft until you see another opening. Click on the grate to open it and drop down inside Gehn's lab.

- ▶ You can now unlock the front door, read Gehn's lab journal, and use the tram out the back door to travel to Plateau Island.

- ▶ Make sure you read the lab journal and make note of the numerical code that's inside it. Remember: You can't take the journal with you!

THE MAP TABLE PUZZLE

- ▶ On Plateau Island, there's a rather fiendish puzzle, easy to work, but difficult to interpret. You must solve this puzzle, however, to complete the Marble Puzzle encountered later.

- ▶ When you ride the elevator up to the mountaintop, you will have access to two areas. First, there's a spot over-looking five plateaus, which represents the five islands of Riven. Second, there's a large, circular building, the Map Room, in the center of a lake. The two sites are con-nected by a path running through the elevator and across a narrow walkway that may extend into the lake.

- ▶ At the overlook, look down to see the control panel, a plate with five buttons, each shaped like the graphic designs representing the five different islands. Push one of the buttons. Note how the plateau below the overlook represent-ing that island changes: water flows onto the top, assuming the shape of 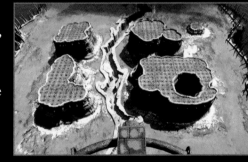 that island's mountainous terrain. (Water on Riven, as you may have noticed by now, does not behave the same way that it does in more mundane universes!)

- ▶ Leaving the button on the control panel down, cross the path from the overlook to the Map Room. The walkway now extends out to the Map Room.

▶ The Map Table is a large grid divided into a five-by-five array of large squares, twenty-five squares in all.

▶ One square on the Map Table represents one square in the small island symbol below.

▶ Elsewhere in your travels—on a plaque inside the entrance to the Great Golden Dome, on the mosaic revealed behind one of the beetles in the Gate Room, and on the control panel at the over-look here on Plateau Island—you have seen small graphic designs representing the five islands of Riven. You will see them again on the linking books to each of the islands. The array before you—the Map Table—represents the same shapes.

▶ When you press one of the island-shaped buttons at the overlook above the plateaus, that island shows the shape of its terrain with oddly flowing water. At the same time, that particular island is displayed here, in the Map Room.

▶ One of the large squares of the island display will be highlighted in yellow. Press that square, or any other, to bring up a holographic image of the terrain in that square. Note the blue lines further dividing the terrain into a five-by-five grid of small squares.

▶ You must conclude that the puzzle requires you to note the locations of each of the Fire Marble Domes on the five islands of Riven, one dome for each island. You should be able to make this deduction when you see the Marble Puzzle in the upper level of the Golden Dome, when you see the 25x25 grid and the six colored marbles to the right. (You will only need five of the six marbles—a further twist to this admittedly fiendish puzzle.)

▶ Next, in each large
  square, we identify the
  small squares by labeling
  the columns across A, B,
  C, D, and E, and numbering the rows down 1, 2,
  3, 4, and 5.

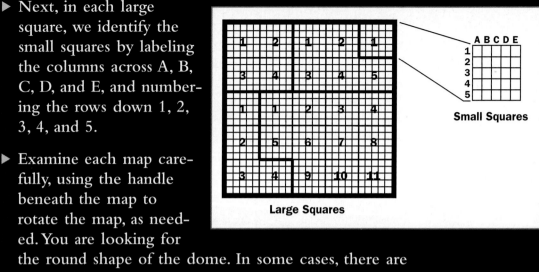

Small Squares

Large Squares

▶ Examine each map care-
  fully, using the handle
  beneath the map to
  rotate the map, as needed. You are looking for
the round shape of the dome. In some cases, there are
identifiable terrain features to guide you.

▶ The Fire Marble Dome on Crater Island (in the
  upper-left corner) is directly beneath a crater or hole
  in a mountain top.

▶ The dome on Plateau Island is just behind a narrow,
  V-shaped cleft in the rock wall of the central lake.

▶ The dome on Temple Island is on a flat bit of land
  extending beyond the circle of the Great Dome.

▶ The dome on Jungle Island is located on a cylindrical
  pillar of stone.

▶ Prison Island's dome is on a spit of land extending
  out into the sea at the northwestern edge.

THE MOIETY AGE

▶ You must reach the Moiety Age at some point in your quest to recover your trap book and to find Catherine's journal.

▶ To open the gateway to the Moiety Age, you need to acquire clues on Jungle Island (plus one missing piece from Plateau Island).

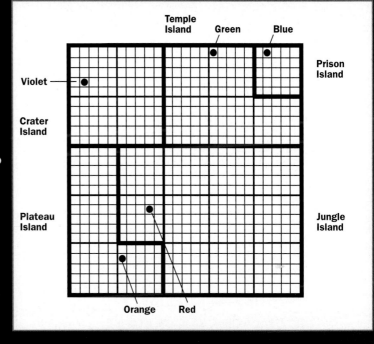

▶ Find the silhouette of a frog near the tram that brings you to Jungle Island. The wooden eye has the D'ni numeral "3" on the back and makes a song like a frog's chirp.

▶ Find the silhouette of a beetle in a stone pool you fill with water on the way to the access ladder at the submarine pen. The wooden eye has the numeral "2" on the back and makes a sound like the whirr-click of a beetle.

▶ Find the silhouette of a wahrk in the rocks on the lagoon past Sunner Rock. The wooden eye has the D'ni numeral "5" and makes a whale-like sound similar to a wahrk. You can confirm this by calling a wahrk and hearing its cry when you are in Gehn's underwater Viewing Chamber on Plateau Island.

The wahrk approaches your vantage point if you use the Color Wheel to turn on the red light outside.

▶ Find the fourth eye in the jungle, off the path just below the spot where a large dagger is thrust point-down into the earth. There is no animal silhouette here, but the eye, which has the numeral "4" on the back, makes the distinctive bark of a sunner—which you have heard if you were able to sneak close to the sunners on their basking rock earlier.

▶ Find the fifth silhouette—of a fish with a vaguely delta-form shape—in the viewer you find on Plateau Island, in Gehn's underwater Viewing Chamber. Although you can see what might be the wooden eye through the viewer, you cannot reach its location. However, you can find a duplicate of this eye in Gehn's lab.

▶ When you reach the Moiety Gateway, a room with a circle of 25 stones, each with the graphic image of a different Rivenese life form, you must touch the five stones in the correct sequence.

▶ The images and the sequence are:

▶ If you click on the wrong stone or in the wrong order, nothing will happen. To back out of a mistake, simply touch the stones again, and then begin again with the correct sequence.

THE FIRE MARBLE DOMES (FIRST STEP)

▶ At some point in your quest, you must enter a different age or world, the place where Gehn resides, a universe he calls "233." (Gehn has been working on a lot of universes! Riven is his fifth!)

▶ You can reach Gehn's world by using the linking book inside any of the Fire Marble Domes you see rotating against the Riven landscape during your explorations.

▶ To open a rotating Fire Marble Dome, you must approach one of the kinetoscopes placed facing the dome and look through the eyepiece.

▶ As you look through the eyepiece, the rotating shutter creates a kind of animation, enabling you to see the changing symbols on the rotating dome blend into a kind of movie. One of the symbols, however, is marked in yellow, and you will see it flash this color as it goes past.

▶ Click the button on top of the kinetoscope to catch the yellow symbol as it appears. This may take some practice and several tries, but keep at it. When you click on the correct symbol, both the rotating shutter and the dome stops. The dome then opens, and for just an instant you will see the linking book inside. Then an inner dome locks shut, a second puzzle that you must solve to link with Gehn's world.

▶ Make sure you sketch or otherwise note the symbol that opens each dome, and remember which island you found it on. The symbols refer to specific colors; you will need to know what color goes with which island to solve the Marble Puzzle later on.

▶ The kinetoscope for the Crater Island Fire Marble Dome is hidden. Closing the door to the Fire Marble Dome chamber reveals a tunnel to the right. The kinetoscope is at the end of that tunnel.

▶ The kinetoscope for the Fire Marble Dome on Plateau Island is broken. You can stop that dome by simply clicking on the switch rapidly (basically just click the mouse as quickly as you can) and catching the appropriate symbol randomly. This method, incidentally, can be used on any of the domes, should you have trouble catching the correct symbol as it flashes past. When you catch the symbol, you will hear a change in the sound made by the rotating shutter, and the device will spin down. A moment later, the dome will open.

▶ Because the kinetoscope is broken, you must determine the correct symbol for Plateau Island by careful observation of the dome while it is still spinning.

THE FIRE MARBLE DOMES (SECOND STEP)

▶ To reach the linking book inside a Fire Marble Dome, you must get the correct five-digit code and use it to position the sliders along the scale on the inner dome lock. When the sliders are correctly positioned, push the button. The sliders will move all the way to the left and the dome will open. If you have the setting wrong, the sliders move to the left, but nothing else happens, and you can try again.

▶ The code is located in Gehn's lab journal, in his laboratory on Crater Island. Note that the code is different each time you play Riven.

▶ The code is a string of five D'ni numerals, and some will be higher than 10. Because the Wahrk Gallows toy in the school room only teaches you the numerals up through 10, you need to figure out how the numbering system works in order to translate higher numbers.

▶ If you have trouble, consult the section earlier in this chapter on D'ni numerals.

▶ The scale on the lock has 25 positions, marked off by fives. Move the right-most slider to the point on the scale corresponding to the highest, right-most number of the code. Move the next slider in line to the next highest number, the second from the right. Continue down the list of numbers, until the last, left-most slider is placed on the last, left-most number in the line.

▶ After entering the correct combination and pushing the button, the inner shield raises and you can access the book. The book will not transport you to Gehn's world, however, unless you have also solved the Marble Puzzle, described later in this chapter, and provided the books with power.

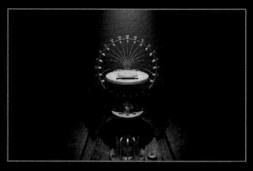

▶ When you use the linking book inside the dome, you will arrive in Gehn's residence in Age 233 (or in D'ni notation, 98). When you use a linking book from this location to a specific island, you will arrive inside the Fire Marble Dome for that island. To exit the dome, move back from the book and click on the button you see on the floor to the right of the book. The dome will open and you will be able to step out.

THE MARBLE PUZZLE

▶ The solution to the Marble Puzzle requires that you solve the Map Table Puzzle on Plateau Island, described earlier in this chapter.

▶ Each of the symbols associated with a different Fire Marble Dome—the symbols used to open the dome with its kinetoscope—represents a color. The colors and symbols, with their respective islands, are as follows:

COLOR	ISLAND
Green	Temple Island
Red	Jungle Island
Violet	Crater Island
Orange	Plateau island
Blue	Prison Island
Yellow	None

Note that you must guess at the color for Prison Island, because you can't reach that Fire Marble Dome until after you have solved the Marble Puzzle. Note, too, that you must guess at the color associated with the Crater Island symbol, because that light (violet) is broken on the Color Wheel.

▶ The Marble Puzzle array, which is obviously based on the map array on Plateau Island, must be mentally divided up into the graphic logos for the five islands.

- Each large island square is numbered, running left to right, top to bottom.

- Each large island square is further divided into a five-by-five grid. For simplicity, mentally label the vertical columns of each A, B, C, D, and E, going left to right, and the horizontal rows 1, 2, 3, 4, and 5, going top to bottom.

- The proper marble placement for each island is as follows:

ISLAND	COLOR	LARGE SQUARE	COORDINATES
Crater Island	Violet	1	B4
Temple Island	Green	2	A1
Prison Island	Blue	1	B1
Plateau Island	Orange	4	A2
Jungle Island	Red	5	D2

- When the marbles are properly placed, move the lever on the wall, and then press the white button. An explosion of air from beneath the marble press signals that power has been provided to the linking books.

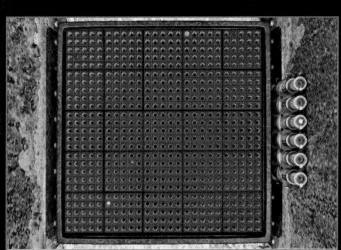

Gehn. It was taken from you when you first arrived in Riven. To get it back, you must solve the puzzle of the Moiety Gateway, enter the Rebel Age, and get the trap book from Nelah, one of Catherine's allies.

▶ In Gehn's residence, while you are behind the bars, Gehn takes the book, which he thinks is a gateway to the world of D'ni. After considering going through, he reconsiders and asks you to go through first.

▶ Although this seems at first glance to be suicide, it is in fact precisely what you must do. Touch the image on the book, and you will find yourself trapped inside. You will see Gehn looking at you... but he is in fact watching a moving image of the subterranean world of D'ni. After a moment, he will touch the image to follow you in.

▶ If you played Myst, you already know how trap books work. When Gehn touches the image, he trades places with you; he is now inside the book, while you are in his home, free to explore outside the bars of your cage.

RELEASING CATHERINE

WARNING! DON'T TOUCH THE IMAGE IN THE BOOK AGAIN, OR YOU WILL ONCE AGAIN TRADE PLACES WITH GEHN—THIS TIME PERMANENTLY!

▶ You can reach Catherine's island only through the linking book in Gehn's residence. First, either Gehn must turn on the power to all of the books before you trap him, or you must turn on the power after you trap him.

▶ Trap Gehn. You can only do this by entering the trap book yourself. When he follows, you exchange places with him, trapping him in the book and leaving you outside of the cage.

▶ Go to the ladder leading down to Gehn's bed chamber. Go to his bedside table and open the gray sphere, which is a kind of timepiece. As it opens, note the progression of clinking sounds.

▶ Go back upstairs and find the lever that lowers the cage around the linking books access.

▶ Go to Catherine's island, using the linking book with the single square. Enter the same sequence of sounds you heard from the gray sphere using the three keys in the elevator and pull the lever.

▶ The bars will open, the elevator will rise, and Catherine, freed at last, will join you.

Position 2 of the Gate Room is turned to point to the right, providing power to the telescope assembly.

- ▶ Enter the numbers to open the hatch on the steel plates beneath the telescope.

- ▶ Move the pin on the support strut at the left, which enables the telescope to go down.

- ▶ Lower the lever, and then press and hold the green button to move the telescope down until the glass is cracked and the Star Fissure is opened.

THINGS *NOT* TO DO IN RIVEN

Although Riven is not a violent or combat-oriented game, there are a few things that you should avoid if at all possible. In some cases, you can even be killed.

- ▶ Do *not* use the trap book yourself when Gehn is not around. You will be trapped there forever, and Atrus will be very upset.

- ▶ When Gehn offers you a chance to touch the trap book image, do *not* continue to refuse him. After three refusals, he will decide to stop wasting time on you and kill you. Well, what did you expect of someone who smokes frogs and plays God with people's lives?

▶ When you trap Gehn, do *not* touch the image of D'ni again! You will exchange places with him once more, and this time, you will be trapped in the book forever.

▶ Do *not* power up and operate the telescope before you have trapped Gehn. If you do, Atrus will appear... and, moments later, so will Gehn, along with one of his guards. Gehn will kill both Atrus and you.

▶ Do *not* operate the telescope before you rescue Catherine. If you capture Gehn but do not free Catherine, you have won a limited and melancholy victory at best... one where you and Atrus have survived, but where Atrus may never see his wife again, and where the Rivenese themselves may all die in a world's collapse. Pity Atrus! He has lost his beloved Catherine, the world he has labored to save, and his father, all at the same time!

Chapter Six

WALKTHROUGH: ALL REVEALED

*This is a Wahrk chapter. Don't read it, don't even page through it
unless you want to have a lot of the fun and mystery of Riven
spoiled for you!*

*This chapter gives away everything, without worrying about how or
where you get much of the information, and with scarcely a nod toward the rich and
atmospheric wonder that is the world of Riven. Follow this outline if you want to get
from beginning to end in the shortest and most direct possible time.*

*A much better idea is to play the game and figure out the puzzles for yourself, or at
most with a little help from other chapters in this book! Then look here to compare
how you did with this walkthrough, and to see what other endings you might have
encountered!*

*Also, with a game like Riven, there is no one right or best way to move among the
various locations or to gather the necessary clues. The order of events in this walkthrough is not the only way to get through the game; it's not even necessarily the best
way. In most cases, what is important is that you assemble the clues and solve the
puzzles—not the order in which you do so.*

▶ When you are released from the cage, check out that mechanism ahead. It's a telescope, but it seems to be pointed at a sealed hatch on a portion of the ground covered by iron plates. Note the lever to the right, with a button in the middle. Neither works. The mechanism has no power.

▶ Go back toward the cage you arrived in and around to the left. Follow the steps up. Briefly, venture out onto the bridge leading to your right, stop, turn, and look back to see the enormous golden dome behind and to the left of the Gate Room. This is your first goal.

▶ Return back the way you came on the bridge and continue straight ahead into the Gate Room antechamber. Note a button on the wall to your right, and the open door ahead leading into the Gate Room. Proceed into the Gate Room.

▶ Explore the Gate Room. It is five-sided, with two open doors, currently at positions 1 (where you came in) and 3, which is blocked by a grating. You must open that grating to proceed through the second doorway at 3, which leads to the giant golden dome. Note the beetles on the pillars. The pull ring at the tail of each beetle reveals a small painting, different for each. A very close look at each of the three walls covered with indecipherable writing reveals tiny pin-holes through the stone.

▶ To use the Gate Room, you must understand its geometry. There are five possible gateways which can be numbered for easy discussion, starting at 1 (on the southeast wall, where you came in), and proceeding clockwise around the room, 2, 3, 4, and 5. Pushing any of the rotation buttons outside the Gate Room rotates the room by one wall (72 degrees).

▶ Go back to the antechamber. You begin with open gates aligned at 1 and 3. Push the button on the right to rotate the Gate Room clockwise 72 degrees. At this point, the gate into the room is closed, but you can peek through a small lens in the recess in front of you and see the room's interior.

▶ The room's open gates are now aligned with positions 2 and 4. Push the rotation button again to turn the gateways to positions 3 and 5. Push it again to turn the gates to positions 4 and 1. The gateway in front of you is now open once more. Note that the gate at position 4 is closed off by a grate.

▶ Push the button to rotate the room one more time. The open gateways should now be at 2 and 5. Go out to the path, turn left, and follow the steps down. When you've gone as far as you can, turn left twice to face a locked gate. Click under the gate to go inside. Go up the ladder and across a board. Ahead, note the open door into the Gate Room at position 5.

▶ Go through the Gate Room and into the cave at position 2. Throw the steam valve lever, which turns on the power to the telescope apparatus outside. (You won't need this until the end of the game, but you might as well take care of this little chore now.) Turn around and head back toward the Gate Room. Note the rotation button to the right of the door, and a lever to the left. Throw the lever to raise the grate closing off position 4.

▶ Push the rotation button twice to open positions 2 and 4. Go through the Gate Room to position 4. The grating is raised now, enabling access to an antechamber at 4, but the way beyond is blocked by a massive door. Obviously, you'll need to go somewhere else to open this door. Turn around to see another handle on the left side of the door. Throw it to lower the grate you originally noticed at position 3.

▶ Push the rotation button twice to move the openings to positions 4 and 1. Go across the Gate Room to

the main entrance and rotate
twice to align positions 1 and
3. With the grate at position
3 now raised, cross the room
to position 3.

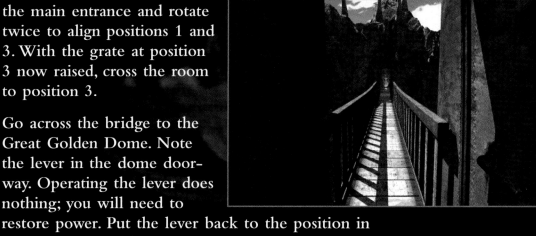

▶ Go across the bridge to the
Great Golden Dome. Note
the lever in the dome doorway. Operating the lever does
nothing; you will need to
restore power. Put the lever back to the position in
which you found it.

▶ Enter the giant chamber. Note the sign, which shows
island symbols and indicates that this chamber connects
with all five. It also shows the catwalk you are standing
on, with a missing piece at 5 o'clock. If you look to
your right, you can see the missing catwalk section, and
what looks like a large wheel on the far side.

▶ Follow the catwalk to the left, going down a long flight
of stairs as you circle halfway around the chamber.
Outside, find a short catwalk extending out from the
main walkway, where a vertical pipe is bleeding off
steam. Throw the steam valve lever to turn power on to
the West Drawbridge (which connects the Golden
Dome with Crater Island). Return to the main catwalk
and follow it to the left. Note the elevator button on
the rock face as you pass, but continue on around the
outside of the giant dome, passing into and through a
rock tunnel. Exit the tunnel to find another steam valve.
Throw the lever to restore power to the bridge connect-
ing the giant dome with the Gate Room.

▶ Turn around and head back through the tunnel. As you
emerge from the tunnel, notice the button set in the
wall to your left. At the moment, it's not operational,
but remember it. You may need it later.

▶ Now return to the Golden Dome and go through it up
the stairs. At the entrance, throw the lever and watch
the bridge raise and extend to a position somewhere
above you. Lower the bridge again and return to the
Gate Room. Go through to position 1. You have now
solved the Gate Room puzzle.

TEMPLE ISLAND: THE TEMPLE

▶ Cross the bridge to the temple area of the island. Go through the entrance and down a passageway. Go to the door on the left of the passageway and enter the Temple Imaging Room. Note the throne in the chamber. The button on the right as you sit in the throne lowers and raises a cage structure over you. The lever on the left probably controls imaging.

▶ From here you can see two small imaging devices. Go to the device to the left of the door and throw the lever up to open a door in a room filled with pillars (the Temple downstairs). Return to the passageway. Go left and down to the Temple by opening a heavy stone door.

▶ Note the throne display set between statues of giant fish-creatures (wahrks) with offerings. Obviously, someone sitting in the throne in the smaller room upstairs can have his image projected into this caged-in throne area in the Temple, an effect that might make him seem godlike in his power.

▶ Turn around to see the open door, just to the left of the hidden door behind the pillars through which you entered the room. Go through the open door and to the right to a mag-lev tramline. Note the blue-lit sphere next to the steps. Press the top to call a tram car to the station when you need one.

▶ Get into the tram. Throw the knob to the left around to the right to rotate the car. Then push the power lever forward to go. You're on your way on a wild ride to Jungle Island.

Jungle Island: From the Sunners to the Submarine

> ▶ When you leave the car, turn to your right. Move forward, then turn right again. Look until you find a small wooden device painted like a crude eye. Rotate the eye and carefully note the symbol carved on the back. Also listen to the creak-chirp sound the eye makes as it turns. Finally, turn around  and go up the stairs directly ahead of you. Partway up, turn around and look back the way you came. Do you see the outline of the tunnel mouth? It's shaped somewhat like a frog... with the wooden Eye appearing in the same relative position as the eye of a real frog.

> ▶ Follow the steps on up. Note the blue light sphere— another tram call button. Go out of the tunnel and down the stone steps. At the cross path, turn left and keep going down.

> ▶ Ahead, note some animals sunning on a rock just below the path. As you approach, they raise their heads and make deep, whuffling noises. Wait until their heads are down and they stop moving, then approach another step, leaving the path and moving slowly down onto the beach. If you move too quickly—if you click to move when their heads are up—you will scare them off.

> ▶ If you move cautiously enough, you will get all the way to the beach, where one of the sunners will raise its head and deliver a loud, distinctive bark. Note the sound. You'll need to remember it later.

> ▶ As long as you're down here, turn right, and then follow the beach around the sunners' lagoon to the left. Note the steps in the distance, but follow the beach to the left as far as you can. Turn around to see the rocks which form the rough shape of the fish-creature—a wahrk—that you saw in the temple, with another wooden Eye.

> ▶ Move out on the sandbar in front of you to reach the Eye. Move it to see another symbol and hear a sound that resembles a whale's call. Note both the symbol and the sound. You'll need to remember them both.

▶ Return to the beach where you saw the sunners. Go back up the rocks to the path and turn left. Follow the path up the steps you saw from the beach and enter the tunnel. Emerge on a rickety wooden walkway and follow it to the end. Up ahead, you can see a guard tower, where a guard is waving something—presumably to give warning— before he disappears.

▶ From here you can look out across an inner lagoon, a lake filling a huge, circular crater. Note a peculiar spherical vehicle on a high ledge to the left. Beyond, you can see a number of strange, spherical buildings.

▶ Go down the ladder. Note a dry pool. Turn the petcock on the right to fill the pool. Note the beetle shape formed by the water, with another wooden Eye. Turn the Eye to note both the symbol and a whirr-click sound. You'll need to remember both.

▶ Go around Beetle Pool and down the ladder. Follow the walkway to the left. Note what look like holes in the water of Village Lake, and various curious structures around the crater's inner walls. Go into a short tunnel. Find a ladder leading down into a hole in the water. You can't go any farther.

▶ Go back up the ladders, back along the walkway, and back past the beach all the way to the T-intersection landing. Go past the landing where you came in, and go up the steps in front of you. At the top, cross a rope-and-plank bridge. Note the clear-cut area and jungle beyond, with gate and paths. Follow the path to the right when it branches, and then take the next left, turning toward a gate. Note a beetle crawling on the gate post. Click on it to hear the sound it makes, a kind of whirr-click you've heard before, when you turned the wooden Eye at the beetle-shaped pool. Go through the gate into the forest.

▶ Follow the path. Go down the steps, and note a volcanic rumbling in the distance. Go through a tree, past luminous fungus.

▶ Turn around and look for a giant dagger. Turn right at the dagger, following the steps down, clicking on the light. See another wooden Eye.

▶ Turn the Eye and hear a sunner bark. Note the symbol. There is no animal silhouette associated with this Eye.

▶ Return to the main path, proceeding left. See the red glow and hear the rumble, louder now. Take the left-hand path at the Y intersection. Go through the gate, turn left, and up the steps to find yourself back in the clear-cut on what had been the left path when you first approached this area. Go back to the gate. Note the turning fire marble. Go back to the Y intersection. Take the left path (the right path when you first approached this Y intersection). Go along the walkway and down.

▶ Ahead, you can see a giant wahrk idol at the end of the path. There is a cunningly hidden switch on top of the post to the right. Click here to raise the switch and open the wahrk idol's mouth, revealing steps leading up.

▶ Follow the steps. Note the tram call and a wooden elevator. Turn around to find the lever that closes the wahrk idol's mouth. Turn back and enter the elevator. Go down, turn around, and follow the blue path to another tramcar station. Go back to the elevator and go up two levels, above the level where you entered the idol's mouth.

▶ Emerge from the elevator on a catwalk high above the forest floor. Follow the walkway, going past a branching to the right to reach another fire marble. Note the colored symbol on the rotating dome Go back to that branch you passed earlier (now on the left) and follow it to a kinetoscope.

▶ Click the top button when the colored symbol appears, or click the mouse button rapidly until you catch the right symbol by chance. Make a note of the symbol—an eye with a vertical line in the pupil.

▶ Return to the dome, now open, and go past it, climbing a flight of steps to a tower. Open the door and go inside. Note the wahrk skull chair.

▶ When you are seated in the throne, the left handle raises and turns the throne, moving it up to a position from which you can look down on Village Lake. Almost directly below is a circular platform beneath a high tower—the wahrk gallows, a place of bloody execution.

▶ Pushing the right handle forward closes the bottom platform on the gallows. Do this. Note the tracks under the water of the lake.

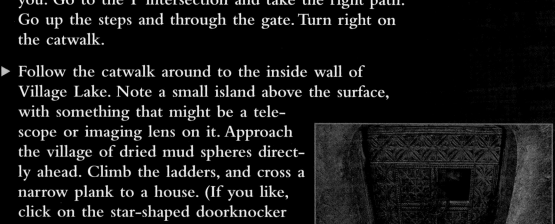

▶ Move the left handle to go back down and leave the room. Go out and back along the walkways to the elevator. Go down one level to the wahrk idol. Push the lever to open the idol's mouth and exit.

▶ Go along the path, toward the tunnel beneath the marble dome, and see a native child run away from you. Go to the Y intersection and take the right path. Go up the steps and through the gate. Turn right on the catwalk.

▶ Follow the catwalk around to the inside wall of Village Lake. Note a small island above the surface, with something that might be a telescope or imaging lens on it. Approach the village of dried mud spheres directly ahead. Climb the ladders, and cross a narrow plank to a house. (If you like, click on the star-shaped doorknocker to knock on the door. You'll catch a glimpse of someone who obviously doesn't want to talk to strangers.)

▶ Follow the walkway to the left, going up a ladder and along the catwalk. Approach a spherical, mechanical contraption—the submarine. Throw the lever on the left to lower the sub into the water. Note the ceremonial area, where large creatures—wahrks, perhaps?—are cut up and their flesh hung up to dry.

► Return along the walkways and ladders. In front of
the house with the plank, look down into the lagoon
to see the sub now resting in a hole in the water, resting on the underwater tracks.

► Follow the walkway all the way back around the lake,
past the gate to the Fire Marble Dome, and up and
out past the clear-cut. Cross the rope bridge, go back
down past the now-empty Sunner Rock, and follow
the paths and ladders past the Beetle Pool and down
and through to the last ladder, which now gives you
access to the lowered submarine. You're ready now for
a drive around the bottom of Village Lake.

JUNGLE ISLAND: THE SUBMARINE CIRCUIT

► Figure out how the controls work. The turning handle
at the center makes the sub change direction; the
lever at the bottom determines which track, left or
right, the sub will take at the next track junction; the
lever at the right moves the vehicle forward to the
next siding or decision point. The gauge at the top
right simply shows when the sub is powered up and
ready to move.

► Turn the sub around, then move forward twice. Look
up, open the hatch, and climb the ladder up to the
Ladder Control Room.

► You will find three lever handles down, two up.
Throw the three handles so that all are up. This
extends all submarine access-ladder bridges around
the lake.

► Return to the sub. Reverse the sub's direction, go forward onto the main track, and then left at the next
siding. Exit the sub and follow the path into the village school room.

► There are several things of interest here, including a
cage with a turn-crank that projects a 3D holographic
image of Gehn. Turn the crank and get a feel for his
evident enjoyment in playing God.

▶ Go to the wahrk hangman game. Moving the ring at the base brings up a random symbol and lowers one of the two hanging figures a certain number of clicks toward the waiting wahrk at the bottom.

▶ The symbols, you now realize, are numbers. You can learn what symbol represents which number by counting the clicks with each turn. Play the game until you have learned all of the D'ni numbers from one to ten.

▶ What do you think of a world where the children play games that randomly sacrifice victims to hungry monsters? Remember, Gehn rules this world!

▶ You now know that the symbols you've been finding behind the wooden Eyes are numbers. The Eye at the frog shape near the tram station was numbered 3. The Eye on the stones that looked like a wahrk was numbered 5. The Eye in the jungle that sounded like the sunner bark was numbered 4. The Eye in the Beetle Pool was numbered 2. This gives you a useful series: Beetle: 2. Frog: 3. Sunner: 4. Wahrk: 5. You do not know what animal might be number 1, nor do you know yet what the sequence is for.

▶ Return to the sub. Reverse its direction and go forward one. Make sure the left track is selected, then go forward once more. Exit the sub at the wahrk gallows.

▶ Cross to the center of the gallows. Pull the triangular-shaped handle to lower a bar. Click on the bar to carry yourself up to the top of the gallows. Pass between the wahrk skulls toward a barred, circular portal. Look inside to see a native being held captive.

JUNGLE ISLAND: FIND THE GATEWAY
TO THE MOIETY AGE

▶ Turn right and follow the walkway to a star-shaped control in the rock. Activate the control and watch the portal open. The native is gone, vanished, it seems, into thin air.

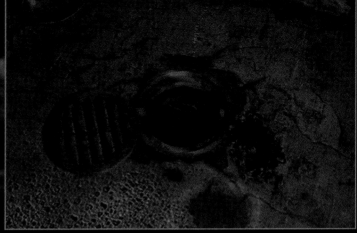

► Click on the drainage grate on the floor. Click on the dirty water beneath the grating to open a secret panel in the back wall of the cell. Go through the opening.

► Go into the tunnel, and hear the door close behind you. Seven clicks in the darkness takes you to a light.

► Click on the branch on the left to turn on a light. Turn around and go up to where you can just see another light. Touch the bulb to turn it on and extend the light further. Move ahead one and touch another light. Move ahead one more to see a door. Move ahead one more and touch the light, then turn to see the door on the right. Opening the door to the right closes the door to the left. Follow the new passage.

► Enter a circle of 25 stone pillars decorated with graphic animal totems. At this point, you do not have enough information to solve the totem puzzle. The sequence Beetle: 2, Frog: 3, Sunner: 4, and Wahrk: 5 might apply here, but you still don't know what the first symbol is. You could try solving it by brute force, trying one animal, followed by the four you know in sequence and then resetting the whole thing and starting all over with another animal as 1, and another, and another. There is a better way, however. Leave it for now.

► Return up the passage to the secret door. Pull the handle to open the secret door. Go back out through the empty prison cell.

► Go to the right out of the prison door. Follow the catwalk. Click on the ladder to lower it to the lower level of the catwalk. Go down the ladder, turn around, and follow the catwalk back clockwise around the lagoon.

▶ Continue along the path and out the gate into the clear-cut area. Take a left, followed by a right, to a square tunnel, and go down the tunnel to the logging car ride. Pull the handle on the left to start the car.

CRATER ISLAND

▶ Arrive at Crater Island and get dumped into a log chipper. Go down the ladder to see a boiler in the distance. Check the ladder behind the chipper on the rock. It leads to a round hatch, which leads in turn to the logging car for a return trip to Jungle Island.

▶ Go past the boiler and follow the beach around the lake counterclockwise to find a very tall, narrow ladder leading to a hatchway far up the side of the cliff. This hatch is locked from this side, meaning you can't get through. Note the building farther down the cliff, along an inaccessible catwalk. This is Gehn's laboratory, your eventual goal.

▶ Go to the long, narrow pier extending out into the middle of the lake. There you will find a valve handle with three possible positions. Turning it to the position farthest to the left powers the log chipper. Turning it to the middle position powers the boiler. Turning it to the right—the position in which you find it—powers the frog-catching apparatus in a cave near Gehn's laboratory. Set the valve to the middle position.

▶ Return to the boiler and check it out. The door won't open, and there's a red light on outside the door.

▶ Go back around the outside catwalk to the right to find the boiler controls. The first lever at the Y junction on your left controls routing of power from the pipe leading out to the middle of the lake. The higher (left) setting powers the pumps that fill or drain the boiler. The lower (right) position powers a grate that can move up or down inside the boiler. Leave the lever on the upper (left) setting.

▶ Turn to the right and examine the boiler controls. The lever at the lower right turns on the heat to the boiler when thrown from an upright to a horizontal position. You hear a roar, as from a furnace. Turn this lever to the upright position and note that the roar stops and the water in the tank stops boiling.

▶ The wheel at the left moves a pipe that enables you to fill or empty the tank with water. Turn the wheel and watch the water level in the tank fall.

▶ A switch at the upper right controls the position of the movable floor grate inside the tank. First turn to your left and switch the power valve from the upper (left) position to the lower (right) position. Then face the controls again and raise the switch to raise the grate.

▶ Return to the door of the boiler. Note that the red light is now off. Open the door and look inside. A tube or drainage pipe descends through the middle of the floor, with a ladder leading down.

▶ Cross the grate and go down into the drain. You will be enveloped in complete darkness. Click five times until you see some light ahead. One more click brings you to a ladder going up. Continue to move toward the light and emerge from a pipe high up on a mountainside above the sea.

▶ Turn left and follow a faint, worn path in the rocks, going over the top of the mountain and down toward the island's central lake. Move toward a railing on a balcony set against the side of the cliff and climb over. Look down and open the round hatch at your feet. That hatch, locked when you tried to open it from underneath, opens to show the long, narrow ladder you climbed earlier, going down to the beach.

▶ Face the cliff to see the double doors. Go through the doors and into the mountain. Turn around and deliberately close the doors, revealing two passageways, one to the right, the other to the left, that are cunningly hidden when the doors are open. You will be returning to these doors shortly.

▶ Turn around again and follow the catwalk into the cave. At the end is an elaborate trap apparatus used by Gehn for catching frogs.

▶ Catching a frog is not necessary for winning the game, at this point, but if you want to try, return to the beach via the precipitous ladder outside,  go to the power control in the middle of the lake, turn the valve back to the right, then return to this chamber. Touch the steel sphere at the top to open the trap. Click and drag to move one of the tiny food pellets from the open container on the right to the trip lever in the middle of the trap. Throw the lever at the left to lower the trap. After waiting about a minute, throw the lever again and raise the trap. If the trap hasn't closed, lower it again and wait a little longer. If the trap has closed, touch the top to open it and note the brightly colored frog inside. Listen to its chirp, which is the same as the chirp you heard at the wooden Eye in the frog silhouette on Jungle Island.

▶ While you're here, look up and note the fan. The loud clattering sound you hear is the noise of the fan running. The ventilator shaft beyond leads to Gehn's laboratory, but you can't get at it while the fan is running.

▶ Go back up the catwalk to the two open passages you found behind the double doors. Go left and follow the steps down to a chamber with another Fire Marble Dome.  Go around the side of the dome and note the lens of a kinetoscope set into the side wall of the cavern, which should give you an idea of where to find it. Look up and note the opening in the roof, a geological curiosity that you will need to remember later.

▶ Close the door to the Fire Marble Dome chamber to reveal another hidden door to the right. Enter this room, find the kinetoscope, and use it to stop the spinning dome. Note the symbol: a circle with a vertical line.

▶ Go back up the stairs, then go straight ahead past the double doors and into the passage you noted earlier to the right of the entrance. Follow the walkway and emerge on the formerly unreachable catwalk high above the lake. Go forward until you find a lever and hear the clattering racket of ventilator fans. Throw the lever to turn off the fans.

▶ Continue following the catwalk. The front doors to Gehn's laboratory are locked. Keep going, following the catwalk around a curve, then out onto a long, high bridge spanning the gulf from Crater Island back to the Great Golden Dome. When you reach a lever at a raised drawbridge, throw the lever to lower the bridge and open the way between Crater Island and the Golden Dome.

▶ Continue into the dome, following the walkway to the left. Pass one open doorway to your left and continue on to the open section of catwalk you noted earlier. Turn the large wheel there to extend the bridge and complete the walkway back to the Gate Room.

▶ Proceed to the doorway through which you first entered the Golden Dome. Throw the lever handle on the right to raise the end of the bridge between the Gate Room and the Golden Dome to a new position in the dome somewhere above your head. Leave it there—you'll need access to this higher level from the Gate Room later.

▶ Before you return to Crater Island, turn off at the side passage you passed by earlier. It leads to a high catwalk that goes around to the right along the outside of the building, but you are stopped by a gap in the walkway. Turn around and press the button on the outer wall to the right of the doorway, and you'll see the catwalk restored as the missing section rises into place.

▶ Continue on the path to a heavy door with a lever to the side. Raise the lever to open the door to position 4 of the Gate Room, the one you couldn't open from the inside before. (This step is not necessary for the

▶ Now return to Crater Island and go past Gehn's lab, past the switched-off controls for the ventilator fans, and back to the double doors. Go through and straight down the catwalk to the frog-catching chamber. Look up and then click on the open ventilator duct to climb inside. Follow the shaft until you reach another ventilator grill, and click on the grating to open it. Drop down into Gehn's laboratory.

▶ Check out his lab. This is where he conducts experiments to determine the proper kind of wood with which to make paper, the proper beetles to make ink, and all of the other details necessary for creating the books that link among the infinity of worlds. At another table, note the paraphernalia he uses for dissecting frogs captured in the cave. An extract from the frogs is placed in small, cylindrical containers and smoked in his elaborate pipe.

▶ Find his lab journal and go through it carefully. Find and record a string of five D'ni numerals. This is the code for opening the inner mechanism of the Fire Marble Domes. At this point, you know the numerals for 1 through 10. You must look for patterns within these numerals to deduce the translation of any numbers higher than 10.

▶ Note, incidentally, that this code is different each time you play Riven.

▶ Examine the round chamber in the center of the room... a stove. Pull the lever to open the door and look inside; there's a partly burned linking book. It doesn't work. Note that in Gehn's journal he says he burns books in the oven when they don't work. He seems to be having some trouble getting things right.

▶ Go to the front door and open it; this unlocks it, so that it will now open from the outside. Close the door, remaining inside the lab, and touch the blue-topped tram-call next to the door. Go to the opposite door and down the steps toward a waiting tram.

PLATEAU ISLAND

▶ Ride the tram to Plateau Island. When you arrive, note the door on the opposite side of the tram from the tram's entrance, but don't do anything about it now. Leave the tram, go out the passageway, and climb the steps. Follow the path through huge, monolithic stones. Approach the titanic building and go up the steps into the portal. Pass the huge, stone plateaus that rise on either side from the surface of a pond, like islands in a sea. Continue through the crevice in the rock face and enter an elevator.

▶ Turn around, push the button, and go up to the map viewing level. Go forward, and look down on the plateaus in the pond you observed a moment ago, now obviously maps of Riven's five islands.

▶ Look at the control with five buttons shaped like the islands of Riven. Note how pressing one button causes water to flow onto the top of the corresponding island plateau and hump itself into a three-dimensional relief of that island's topography.

▶ Turn around, walk back the way you came all the way through the elevator to another crater lake. In the middle of the lake is a large structure: the Map Room.

▶ Approach the map chamber. As you cross the causeway, look to the left and note the Fire Marble Dome for Plateau Island turning just beyond a narrow, V-shaped cleft in the rock wall of the crater.

▶ Enter the map room and go up to the central dais. Note that the water maps and plateaus outside correspond to the map currently visible here. Press the yellow square to see a 3D relief of that one square. Use the handle at the bottom to rotate the 3D map so that you can view it from all sides.

▶ Each island is divided into squares, in patterns you have seen before on Temple Island. For example, Crater Island is represented by four squares arranged in a square, while Plateau Island consists of four squares arranged in an L shape.

▶ Each square, when you click on it, can be further divided into a five-by-five square grid. Use various clues acquired so far to deduce where on each 3D island map that island's Fire Marble Dome is located.

▶ For example, by closely examining the upper-left large square of Crater Island, you can locate the hole or crater that you saw earlier when you looked up inside that island's Fire Marble Dome chamber. On Plateau Island, you can identify the V-shaped cleft in the rock wall, while on Jungle Island, you can find the cylindrical stone pedestal on which that island's Fire Marble Dome was built. On Temple Island, you must find the spot on the north side of the island where the dome is built. On the single square representing

Prison Island, which you have not yet been able to visit, you must examine the topography and guess where that island's dome is located.

▶ Use the five-by-five grids to create coordinates for each dome site. For example, if the columns across are labeled A, B, C, D, and E, and the rows down are labeled 1, 2, 3, 4, and 5, then the coordinates of the dome on Crater Island are B-4. Record all of the dome sites—or your best guesses—for later reference.

▶ Leave the map room and go to the junction of catwalks, turning right. Investigate the dome in the cleft. Note, if you can, the symbol highlighted in color—a circle with a horizontal line.

▶ Go back around the catwalk, following its curve counterclockwise. As you walk, observe the wahrk totems rising from the lake and note their colors: blue (visible from the side of the lake near the dome), yellow, orange, and green (closest to the kinetoscope).

▶ The kinetoscope is broken, the device pushed out of alignment. To open the dome, simply click your mouse button rapidly until it stops.

▶ Return to the elevator, and ride it down to the plateau. Walk along the path, noting the three-dimensional water mountains still rising above the last island you examined. Return to the tram. Rotate the tram in order to get out on the side of the door you noticed when you first arrived. Go through the door.

▶ Walk down an orange-lit passageway. Note the handle with yellow stripes on the left just before the hexagonal pool. Throw the lever to raise a golden elevator cage. Go inside. Turn around and push the button to close the elevator and descend beneath the surface of the water.

▶ Emerge from the elevator and follow the passageway through caverns and tunnels. Up ahead, you see Gehn's scribe look up, startled, and dash into a side passage. Follow him, arriving at another tram station in time to see the scribe making good his escape.

▶ Go back to the main passage and turn left. Follow it through a portal and up a long, long flight of steps to enter Gehn's underwater Viewing Chamber.

▶ Sit in the throne. Push the button on the control to the right to rotate and elevate the throne.

▶ Lower the right-hand lever in front of you to bring down the Color Wheel. Look down at the wheel. Note the symbols, some of which are the same as the symbols you've been noting on each of the Fire Marble Domes. Click on either the symbols or the tabs with finger holes to rotate the wheel. Click on the button at the bottom position to turn on an underwater light.

▶ Go through all of the symbols to connect each symbol with a specific color. The lights are located on the underwater portions of the wahrk totems you noticed earlier. One light, the one symbolized by a circle with a vertical line, is broken, and you will need to guess its color.

▶ The vertical eye shape with a dot, a symbol you've not seen so far, is blue. The circle with a dot is green. The horizontal eye with a dot in the middle is yellow. The circle with a horizontal line is orange. The eye with a vertically-aligned, slit pupil is red.

▶ When you click on red, your view shifts up. The red light is visible through the glass of the Viewing Chamber. Wait a few moments in order to see and hear a live wahrk. Apparently, he's trained to come when

the light is on to get food; when he doesn't get food, he will leave. If you want to play with the wahrk's mind, try calling him three more times, and watch him get more agitated each time. After his fourth appearance, he will slam into the glass and then vanish. He will not reappear unless you return considerably later.

▶ Raise the Color Wheel. Pull the lever to lower the left-hand viewer. This one has only two buttons and six tabs with finger holes. Press the button on the left to see a spy-camera view of Catherine in her prison. When this view is active, the finger-hole tabs do nothing.

▶ Press the right-side button to get a camera's view from Village Lake on Jungle Island. Use the tabs to rotate the view, which shows the village, the piers, and the lake's rock walls.

▶ Note one view that looks like the silhouette of a fish created by a rock cavern and its reflection in the water, which resembles the shape of a delta-wing configuration. Note a white speck at the pointed end and surmise that the shape is the missing fifth animal silhouette, and that the white speck—unreachable—is the silhouette's wooden Eye.

▶ Leave the throne and go back down the stairs to the tram car room where you saw the scribe escape. Take the tram car and ride it back to Jungle Island.

THE MOIETY AGE

▶ Leave the tram and go through the open door. Go to the wooden elevator. Ride up one level to the inside of the Jungle Island fish idol.

▶ Leave the jungle via the wooden gate and turn right. Follow the wooden catwalk through the blue-lit cavern and out to the lakeside, where a ladder was lowered earlier. Climb up the ladder. Go to the prison cell and go inside. Open the drain grate, pull the ring, open the secret door and descend into the cavern. Go down the tunnel to the side passage and the room with 25 stones and animal totems.

▶ Touch the stones in the correct order: delta-shaped fish, beetle, frog, sunner, and wahrk. This drains the water

▶ Pick up the Trap Book, but don't use it. Examine the journal, noting the entry about a pin that locks the telescope, and also a series of five D'ni numbers. Later, Nelah returns with a linking book. Touch the linking image to return to the room with 25 stones.

▶ Leave the Moiety gateway tunnel. If the lights are out, just keep clicking to get to the trap door. Pull the ring to exit. Go to the right to the end of the catwalk and go down the ladder. Turn around and follow the catwalk into the cavern, through the blue-lit cave, and past the jungle and clear-cut area. Return to the tram, which takes you back to Temple Island. Go through the Temple, up the passageway, and across the bridge to the Gate Room.

▶ Push the rotation button to set the doorways to positions 1 and 3. Go through to position 3, where the ramp beyond now extends upward to a vertical slit high in the Great Golden Dome. Cross the ramp and enter a high, narrow passageway. Note a lever on the wall, and beyond, the Marble Puzzle.

▶ Look at the marble grid. Six different-colored marbles are lined up to the right. The grid is a five-by-five array of squares further divided into smaller squares, exactly like the array you saw in the Map Room on Plateau Island.

▶ Place five colored marbles in the appropriate spots, based on what you learned in the Map Room and at the Color Wheel. The color is determined by the symbol that opened each dome. The positions are determined by consulting your notes from your session in the Map Room.

▶ When you think you have it right, step back and throw the switch on the wall. The marble press lowers. Push the white button on the wall switch when it appears. An explosion and whooshing sound signals that the marbles are set correctly. You have now powered up the linking books in all of the Fire Marble Domes.

▶ If there is no whooshing sound, the marbles were positioned incorrectly. Go back and try again. You must guess at one of the colors, as well as at the position of the dome on the fifth island. Experiment until you get the right setting.

▶ Return to the Gate Room and go through to entrance 1. Press the rotation button three times to set the gates to positions 1 and 4.

▶ Go through 4 and follow the catwalk beyond. Go into the golden dome. Turn left on the catwalk and cross the walkway extension. Pass the entrance to position 3 of the Gate Room and go down the steps to the Golden Dome's lower level catwalk. Exit the door and follow the walkway to the right past the power valve for the West Drawbridge. Stop on a red plate on the path and turn right. Push the button to take the elevator down a level. Turn and follow the tunnel to some steps leading up. Go up to the Fire Marble Dome.

▶ You now have the five numbers for the dome lock settings from Gehn's lab journal. Move the sliders to the appropriate numbers on the scale and push the button, opening the inner dome and raising the linking book. Open the book and touch the scene inside to travel to Gehn's universe.

GEHN'S WORLD

▶ You arrive inside a cage. Note the link-ing books, each with a graphic symbol of a different island. Turn until you see a button on a star-shaped design mounted on the bars. Touch it to call Gehn and have him talk to you. He talks about being trapped on Riven without books, but you know he has been writing books. He tells you that he is a changed man who wants to atone for the trouble he's caused.

▶ He also smokes frogs and wears a grand version of the uniform worn by the guard who first greeted you upon your arrival. You know about his use of wahrks to instill fear in the natives, and—if the elaborate native warning network and Moiety rebellion are any indication—that the natives are, indeed, terrified of him. All suggest that Gehn is not to be trusted.

▶ He asks you to go through the trap book first, so he can satisfy himself that it is, indeed, a linking book to D'ni as he believes. When he holds the trap book in front of you, click on the picture and get trapped inside the book. Watch while Gehn decides to follow you to D'ni. He gets trapped, you are freed, and you are now inside his home outside of the cage.

▶ Find the switch that turns on the power to the other linking books in the room, and move it to the right.

▶ Find a lever next to a window, and pull it to lower the bars to your former cage.

▶ Find a tunnel leading down and descend a ladder to Gehn's bedroom. Examine the various artifacts there. Go to the bedside table. Examine his personal journal.

- ▶ Click on the gray metal sphere on the table, which appears to be some kind of watch. Listen to the sequence of sounds, which are the code to Catherine's prison.

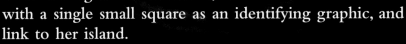

- ▶ Go back up the ladder to the main room. Go into the cage area. Find the book linking to Prison Island, the one with a single small square as an identifying graphic, and link to her island.

CATHERINE'S PRISON

- ▶ Arrive inside the Fire Marble Dome on Catherine's island. Press the button on the floor to the right of the book to lower the book stand and open the dome. Turn and follow the walkway toward a gigantic tree stump covering the entire small, rocky island. Go up the stairs and through a door to an elevator. Note three keys and a lever, plus a pull cord. Press the keys and listen to the different sounds. Enter the correct sequence of sounds, (the sequence you heard on the watch in Gehn's bedroom), then throw the lever to open the cage.

- ▶ Catherine joins you and pulls the elevator handle to descend. She congratulates you. "We're all free! You captured Gehn!" She tells you to go open the fissure and reminds you that the combination is in her journal.

- ▶ Go back to Gehn's residence. You'll have to stop the dome again because Catherine has just used it.

END GAME

- ▶ In Gehn's home, use the book for Temple Island to return there. Go through the tunnel to the elevator and press the button to take you up one level. Go through the Golden Dome to the Gate Room. Go through position 1 and turn right, going down the stone steps.

main controls and pull the lever to the right of the scope down. Press and hold the green button.

▶ Repeatedly press the button until the glass breaks.

▶ Watch Riven destroy itself. Atrus comes through from the chamber in which you first arrived on the island. Catherine arrives a moment later and they embrace. Catharine tells you the villagers are all safely in the Rebel Age. "The path home is now clear for all of us."

▶ Atrus has brought a linking book. Catherine goes through to safety first. He then links through himself, letting the book fall into the fissure. You follow, falling into the Star Fissure...on your way home at last.

RIVEN: THE LOST EPISODES

With the help of this game guide, of course, you made it all the way through Riven without a single mistake or wrong turning. Would you like to see how the game ends if you didn't perform so brilliantly?

Restore to a saved game, made just before the final few moves of play.

YOU FAIL TO TRAP GEHN

If you fail to trap Gehn before opening the Star Fissure, you have lost the game. Atrus will arrive and ask you where Catherine is... and the book. As a dawning horror appears on his features, he says, "I don't understand!"

"You never did!" cries Gehn, appearing behind him with a guard. As the world begins to crumble, Atrus is killed by a blowgun dart.

Gehn retrieves the linking book—his gateway back to D'ni, and freedom—then walks close to you, smiling. "I don't know what you thought you were doing," he says, vastly amused, "but... thank you!" Gesturing with the book, he adds, "I finally am... free..."

He then signals the guard, who shoots you with a blowgun dart.

You fall into darkness as a world dies...

The shock and grief on his face when he realizes that Catherine may be lost forever should spur you on to return to the world of Riven again, this time to end the quest on a less tragic note.

For now, though, the wind howls as a world and a people die.

Make sure that you both trap Gehn in the Book and release Catherine from her prison, using the code in Gehn's bedroom, and you won't have to experience either of these unpleasant endings!

Good luck, and happy adventuring!